Y tú ¿qué hora traes?

Y tú ¿qué hora traes?

Unpacking the Privileges of Dominant Groups in México

By

Ana C. Lopez

BRILL
SENSE

LEIDEN | BOSTON

All chapters in this book have undergone peer review.

The Library of Congress Cataloging-in-Publication Data is available online at http://catalog.loc.gov

Typeface for the Latin, Greek, and Cyrillic scripts: "Brill". See and download: brill.com/brill-typeface.

ISBN 978-90-04-41434-1 (paperback)
ISBN 978-90-04-41435-8 (hardback)
ISBN 978-90-04-41953-7 (e-book)

Copyright 2020 by Koninklijke Brill NV, Leiden, The Netherlands.
Koninklijke Brill NV incorporates the imprints Brill, Brill Hes & De Graaf, Brill Nijhoff, Brill Rodopi, Brill Sense, Hotei Publishing, mentis Verlag, Verlag Ferdinand Schöningh and Wilhelm Fink Verlag.
All rights reserved. No part of this publication may be reproduced, translated, stored in a retrieval system, or transmitted in any form or by any means, electronic, mechanical, photocopying, recording or otherwise, without prior written permission from the publisher.
Authorization to photocopy items for internal or personal use is granted by Koninklijke Brill NV provided that the appropriate fees are paid directly to The Copyright Clearance Center, 222 Rosewood Drive, Suite 910, Danvers, MA 01923, USA. Fees are subject to change.

This book is printed on acid-free paper and produced in a sustainable manner.

For Valeria, my sister, my first friend

Contents

Acknowledgements IX
Introduction X

1 **Positionality and Social Class** 1
  1 The Middle Class 3
  2 Meritocracy 7
  3 Documented in the United States 8
  4 The Value of English 14
  5 Classist Depictions of Underprivileged Populations 16

2 **A Catholicism I Know** 19
  1 Class and Catholic-isms 19
  2 Diversity? 20
  3 Our Bigotry towards LGBTQ+ Groups 22
  4 *Temor de Dios*: The Fear of God 26
  5 *Dios Me Ve* 30
  6 Between Silence and Sexuality 31
  7 *La Culpa* 36
  8 Religious Schooling and Sexuality 38

3 **Imposed Gendered Roles** 42
  1 *La Familia es Primero* 44
  2 Marianismo and Machismo 46
  3 A Feminism That Does Not Work for Everyone 57

4 **Racism in Mexico: *Ojos que no ven, corazón que no siente*** 62
  1 Xenophobia *en Nuestra Casa* 66
  2 Ethnocentrism and Anti-Indigeneity 67
  3 Humor and Media: Time for Accountability 70
  4 The Influence of Media: Present and Past 72
  5 Our Education 75

5 **Ableism** 79

6 **Towards a New Light** 86

References 89

Acknowledgements

I am grateful to Dr. Orelus for encouraging me to write up a proposal for this book during the first year of my doctoral program. Next, thanks to Dr. Flores Carmona for reading this entire *capirotada* with a critical eye, for sharing pertinent readings, resources and powerful conversations regarding accountability and intersectionality. Germain, Valeria, and Anaid, thank you for taking the time to read my drafts while you juggled your own life responsibilities, as well as for your love and support throughout this process. To my faculty advisor, Dr. Salas, for understanding and respecting my desire of engaging in this form of creative writing, while supporting and mentoring me during my doctoral program obligations.

Introduction

Tú qué horas traes? [What time is it on your clock?] is a common saying in Mexico to ask people to look at their own mistakes before pointing them out in others. For example, if I complain about my students' tardiness, but am unpunctual in my own commitments, they might ask me *"Tú qué horas traes?"* Thus, the purpose of this saying is to invite self-reflexivity, self-critique and accountability.

This book is a collection of essays based on narrative in which I recount some of my lived experiences. I share these lived experiences with the purpose of unpacking privilege, while exposing the toxicity of privileged groups in Mexican society. When I use the concept of toxicity I refer to behaviors in which we engage (consciously and unconsciously) that are harmful towards vulnerable groups in Mexico such as Indigenous communities, immigrants, refugees, Black people, non-white Mexicans, non-Mexican Latinx's, low-income and working class populations, and LGBT individuals. As I attempt to unpack some of the problematic behind the multiple forms of oppression enacted in Mexico by individuals with privilege, I start with myself, my family, and the education system as I have experienced. In this text, I have included some of the toxic understandings that we, privileged Mexicans (in Mexico), carry with ourselves because of our failure to challenge our education and inherited nationalist values.

Although there are Mexicans all over the world, here I am referring to Mexicans who are privileged in many aspects of their/our lives, and live in Mexico, particularly in Ciudad Juárez, a northern border city. I have lived most of my life in Mexico. Therefore, the anecdotes and analyses portrayed throughout these pages describe my lived experiences and my witnessing of the different forms of oppression enacted by privileged groups in Mexico. This volume represents but a very small fraction of the problems and social injustices that are perpetuated in my country on a daily basis. My hope is to continue to grow my understanding of the issues that I present here and to continue working from a self-reflective perspective.

1   Who Is "We"?

Throughout this book, I will speak in first-person point of view, telling my personal experiences to illustrate or exemplify some of the topics to be discussed. However, throughout these pages, I will use words like we/us/our, as I point out problematic behaviors, toxic values, and actions that disempower vulnerable populations. When I say "we" I dare to speak for the people that occupy a position of privilege in Mexico, across levels and contexts, as I move forward and talk about personal experiences, I refer specifically to the Mexican northern border, as it is where I have lived most of my life. I say "we" to refer to different groups of Mexicans who share identity privileges: the documented (the commuters with tourist visas who do not need to overstay them as a means of survival, as well as those with work visas who embody privilege in both countries), White and White-passing, bilingual by choice, non-Indigenous, cisgender, heterosexual, Catholic, and able-bodied.

Although the middle and upper classes in Mexico have different layers and levels of complexity, *we* perpetuate and replicate forms of marginalization from our positions in different ways. Therefore, in a country presenting as much inequality as Mexico does, the middle and upper classes of the country replicate the same forms of oppression on different scales. Sharing different privileges, which intertwine with several of our identities, entails a collective responsibility for the multiple ways in which different forms of oppression have been enacted towards vulnerable communities.

When you read "we," you should know I'm speaking about Mexicans who, for way too long, have refused to examine how we use our privileges. When I say "we" I am referring to the Mexicans who live under the comfortable state of "the majority," and who for a long time have had the power to define which values, identities, norms, and ways of living are acceptable and which ones are not. If you are Mexican and possess the above-mentioned privileged identities, but cannot relate or identify with any of the problematic situations that keep social injustices alive in Mexico, congratulations on being one in a million.

CHAPTER 1

Positionality and Social Class

> Every person experiences either privilege or disadvantage on the basis of class position as shaped and complicated by race and racism, gender and sexism, ability or disability and ableism, youth or elder status, ageism or adultism, religion, and religious oppression.
> ADAMS (2013, p. 148)

∴

The Secretary of Social development in Mexico, SEDESOL, states that poverty includes those individuals who "experience scarcity in at least one of these areas: educational, health care, social security, housing and/or nutrition, and their income is not sufficient to acquire the goods and services required to fulfill their nutrition needs" (SEDESOL, 2013, p. 15). Furthermore, according to the Mexican Census Bureau, also known as the INEGI, only 1.7% of the Mexican population has been identified as wealthy, whereas 39.2% are middle class. The majority, which is 59.1%, has been identified as low-income (INEGI, 2013a). Based on these statistics, it is evident that there is a problem with the distribution of wealth in Mexico. What are the numbers telling us? Are the wealthiest 1.7% of the population just working harder than everybody else? Is more than half of the country refusing to progress?

As appointed by Loza (2015), modern Mexico faces several social inequalities. The wealthiest families are a small group and the volume of their wealth increases over time. Meanwhile, families who live on the poverty line in Mexico cannot afford the coverage for the most essential needs. They experience marginalization, and still die of starvation and curable diseases. Such inequalities have come to define the social structures in Mexico (Saraví, 2016). Because we are more benefited than negatively affected by an inequitable system, we have done a very poor job challenging those inequalities. This is especially true when we occupy one of the multiple levels that compose the middle and upper classes. It has become convenient for the privileged Mexican population to normalize poverty as a *triste realidad* [sad reality] because doing so allows us to detach from the problem.

Social Class is one of the greatest dividers of Mexican society (Saraví, 2016; Moreno, 2017). We have learned to construct our social class identity by subscribing to a certain group and concomitantly separating ourselves from others. Individuals are likely treated on the basis of how they look and what they possess. "We are socialized into a system of oppression through interactions, institutions and culture. We learn to accept systems of oppression as normal through interactions with parents, peers, teachers, and other influential individuals in our lives…" (Hardiman, Jackson, & Griffin, 2013, p. 28). Classism is one of those accepted systems of oppression.

From a young age, we learn biased lessons regarding the privileges of the higher classes. We learn that the people who belong to the most powerful groups are educated, speak "proper Spanish," and are White or White-passing. Higher classes, are portrayed as aspirational, and they look White—the dream portrayed in the small and big screens (Navarrete, 2016; Jones, 2019). When I use the term aspirational, I also refer to the way in which these groups are portrayed and perceived; powerful and respectable individuals who "work harder than everybody else and have earned everything they have," and therefore, we should all strive for such a successful life.

Being educated in a private school, having access to technology, traveling for leisure, access to healthcare, and many other material resources position individuals in Mexico in the middle and upper class scope. These often-unchallenged privileges also contribute to the construction of our identities and our perceptions about, and labeling of, others. Education, wealth, and many other resources serve to position us somewhere in the socioeconomic ladder that is Mexico. From the middle and upper-class end, there is such a negative narrative and perception towards poverty and marginalized communities that we do not want to blend or associate with. We keep acting as if the roots of injustice and class inequities were somewhere beyond our reach and responsibility. We do not want to be confused for someone who is experiencing need, as the concept and privileges tied to class entails a position of power. Oftentimes we jokingly say "I am poor" or "I am broke" as an expression to say that our budget is tight. We mindlessly bring up the concept of poverty into trivial conversations without really reflecting upon it, upon our roles and responsibilities in issues of injustice. Nevertheless, when the time comes to identify ourselves, to identify our socioeconomic status, we are *middle class*. We brag about how hard we work and how much progress we have achieved.

1   The Middle Class

According to the Mexican Census Bureau, the middle class in Mexico is made up of approximately 39.2% of the population (INEGI, 2013b). This group is located in the middle of extreme socioeconomic disparities—citizens who aspire to remain in their class positionality, have access to private services and technology, and can obtain growth to some extent. One of the main goals of the middle class is separating itself from the lower classes; the aspiration is always to move up and become a part of the higher classes. Given the enormous inequities that exist between the most powerful classes in Mexico and those who live in the margins of poverty, the Mexican middle class is a very diverse group. For instances, an upper-middle-class family has more access to income, leisure, and technology than a middle-class family who has more proximity to the working-class (Alva, 2015). Yet, regardless of where in the middle-class span we are located, people within this scope definitely have more financial stability than working-class and low-income individuals. According to de-la-Calle and Rubio (2010), Mexican citizens who earn 3–10 times the minimum wage, which is about 4.70 dollars, are considered to be middle class. Such a wide range in earnings translates to a diverse span of opportunities for individuals in the middle class. For example, different earnings are tied to access to different opportunities for education, privilege, and cultural capital. Those families who earn three minimum wages may not have access to a private education, but can afford, with struggle, the most basic services that the less privileged classes are denied.

The middle class is particularly impacted by the agency of more powerful classes in Mexico, as services become privatized, prices increase, and the middle class has to figure out ways of coping and holding their status. Despite the difficulties of navigating the changes in the economy, middle-class citizens in Mexico hold the privilege of having choices. Such privilege has been granted to them by access to education, positionality, and cultural capital (Mantsios, 2013).

According to Loza (2015) cultural capital is a set of skills, knowledge, and experiences that are related to the dominant cultures in a given society. In Mexico, cultural capital is an affordance of the upper and middle classes. For instance, being in the middle class often allows enrollment into private schools, traveling, the acquisition of technology, and other resources and experiences. Furthermore, the affordance of an education, though it is not always of quality, will provide the *prestige* and political skills to succeed in a capitalist society (Tapia & Valenti, 2016). This, in turn, allows many of the middle and upper classes to maintain their/our position in the socioeconomic ladder. Yet, as costs increase and educational and health services become privatized, the cost of living becomes higher, and several families in the middle-class hustle to remain there.

The upper classes in Mexico are guaranteed to afford the expenses of the private schools in the country. Furthermore, private schools in Mexico often work as businesses. As such, they highlight their schools as places to become proficient with technology and to acquire a second language as marketing strategies to increase enrollment and raise the tuition fees. Moreover, technological savviness and English as a second language are valuable skills that not everyone in Mexico has access to (Dossier político, 2006). Because of what the private education in Mexico claims to offer, many families, strive to place their children in these institutions, knowing that they will acquire valuable assets that will allow them to keep their positionality of privilege.

According to Velasco (2016b), among many other forms of marginalization, formal education oftentimes replicates segregation by letting racism, classism, xenophobia, and ethnocentrism permeate the curriculum, tuition rates, and agenda. This becomes more evident in the private education sector (Balderas, 2017). For instance, most billboards that advertise private schools in Ciudad Juárez display White children manipulating computers and wearing neat pricy uniforms with the school symbols. A marketing slogan implies that they will be the bosses and entrepreneurs that Mexico needs.

Although I did not always enjoy the advantages of a middle-class household, because of my father's identities, work, and academic preparation, I was able to experience a gradual transition towards a middle-class positionality. My father comes from an upper-middle-class family and had the opportunity to attend a prestigious college in Mexico. My father struggled to find employment at the beginning of his career, and was reluctant to seek support from his family. He had just married my mother and, because of the economic crises of that time and a lack of job opportunities, they sought work opportunities in areas that were not related to their academic careers. My father is a dentist, and my mother has an incomplete undergraduate education.

After marrying my mother, my father had to work baking bread for a company that catered to a popular Mexican airline for almost 10 years. My parents were both in their 20s when they got engaged. They had no experience and no money in the bank to open a dental office. Therefore, their first career options were narrow and consisted of long hours of work. We lived in multiple rented homes, and were asked to leave once. Luckily, my godmother received us in her apartment for a long period of time while my parents achieved financial stability. We stayed with her until they were able to find a new rental place to live in. Although we moved from one house to another one, we never considered ourselves homeless; there were always opportunities for us to find a place to live or family members that were supportive and helped out in any way they could. Unlike the most vulnerable groups in Mexico, we never had to live in a shelter or on the streets.

I consider myself privileged because I cannot recall much of this time period in our lives, mainly because in spite of the hardships, my parents were always able to feed us, dress us and provide us with an education. Although both of my parents recall the beginning of their marriage as a difficult time in our lives, they acknowledge that as a family, we have many advantages that allowed us to slowly but steadily move up the socioeconomic ladder. Even when resources were scarce, we had many more opportunities than other vulnerable groups in Mexico because we had the advantages of a college education degree, whiteness, familial support, and other resources that allowed my family to navigate economic scarcity.

Despite the struggles and challenges faced by my parents, they were able to afford private elementary and secondary education for me and a private elementary education for my sister. An economic crisis affected my father's income, and there was an increase in the tuition rate at my sister's school, which my parents could no longer afford. This situation forced my parents to find a public school for her. However, despite the struggles and obstacles imposed by an inequitable system, and relatively scarce opportunities for a couple of new graduates in the 90's, my sister and I still had access to privilege. This was granted through a bilingual education that opened doors for us. I do not disparage the hard work of both of my parents, but I also cannot deny the existence of certain conditions, identities, positionality, education, and privilege that helped them navigate the challenges and transition into a stable socioeconomic position.

Being a White Mexican family, in which the providers for the family have college degrees, has a tremendous influence in such transitions. In the middle of the uncertainty posed by the political climate, corrupt governments, crisis, and currency fluctuations, my parents and many of their friends from college had opportunities to grow economically and navigate the system successfully. At the end of the day, corrupt or not, the systems and hierarchies in Mexico ended up working for my family. None of our identities have been threatened by the ruling hierarchies and the government faulty structures.

Even in the presence of multiple economic crises, we took family road trips across the state and to the closest beaches. We stayed in cheap hotels, but enjoyed the comfort of leisure time that my father's work as a dentist allowed. As time passed by, I noticed that our economic growth was occurring really slowly. I noticed this by comparing myself to other children who I shared educational spaces and extra-curricular activities with. Even though we belonged to the same systems and shared spaces, some of them were enjoying expensive vacations all over Europe and had access to the latest technology. Others would have to stay in daycare after school because their mothers worked two shifts in order to pay for their private school tuition.

After being diagnosed with epilepsy at age seven, the doctor told my parents that it would be appropriate for me to take an extra-curricular class in which I could practice coordination. Doing so would supposedly improve my cognitive development. My mother was too overprotective and scared to enroll me in swimming classes, and she found a dance school that I could attend twice a week. I started learning about the relationship between social classes when most of the girls from my dance class refused to engage in conversations with me or interact in any way that did not pertain to the class. We had nothing to talk about, there could not be a connection because although we shared the same space, our experiences and education were very different. Most of my dance peers attended expensive private schools in Juarez and El Paso, traveled globally, and had several material goods that their upper-class status allowed. I had one friend in the nine years of my life I spent there. Most girls would not interact with me because we did not share the same experiences or spaces outside of those four walls. I also did not force the interactions, as I knew we were different. I am not using this example to illustrate marginalization or to portray myself as a victim of classism. However, it is important to me to identify how class has played a role in my interactions with peers throughout spaces and most importantly, how I, too, replicated exclusion in different settings.

> The problem is that privilege isn't something that can be turned on or off. While money can be laid aside unused, privilege is deeply embedded in our lives. It's a part of the experiences that make us who we are, that shape how we see the world and the way the world sees us. Class privilege even becomes a part of our bodies, from straight teeth to a "firm" handshake. (Pittelman & Resource Generation, 2013, p. 221)

In elementary school, we were constantly reminded of how we were better educated because our school was Catholic and private. I internalized the belief that the discipline and religious education I was receiving made me morally superior and *better* than those who were being educated in non-Catholic religions and in public schools. Our teachers would use public schools as an example of chaos and misbehavior, telling us how "children in public schools are messy, disobedient, loud, and misbehaved all the time." They warned us that we should never act that way. For years, I kept this lesson intact. In my ignorance—willful ignorance—I had silently internalized the belief that I was a better person solely because of the education I was receiving. I say silently because nobody ever talks about it openly. In Catholic religious environments, it is oftentimes loudly claimed that everyone is equal towards God's eye. Yet, Catholic schools as mine are guided by classist, discriminatory and condescending principles towards poverty and social injustice. We were all comfortable with a narrative in which our privilege is not more than a blessing or God rewarding us for being "faithful Catholics."

I did not bother to challenge what I was learning in school about poverty and about privilege masked as "being blessed," and meritocracy. I really believed that poverty was a choice and wealth was a product of hard work. During my adolescence and early adulthood, I never really stopped to think about how I contributed to oppression—that is a privilege that only a few get to experience. I saw our transitions through economic struggles unfold and get better gradually, therefore I assumed that every individual counted on the same opportunities. I never considered my own privileges or advantages, because as many of the White middle-class Mexicans, I experienced the comfort of smooth and steady transitions. And for the most part, I was able to live my life occupying spaces in which the majority of the population fits and is accepted.

2   Meritocracy

> Members of oppressor groups, on the other hand, are often unaware of themselves as members of privileged groups because the system of oppression enables them and encourages them to view the accomplishments and achievements of their group members as deserved. (Hardyman, Jackson, & Griffin, 2013, p. 29)

It is common of the middle class to engage both a narrative and mindset in which socioeconomic inequalities are not our problem. We commonly use the argument that we have struggled to earn everything we have as something that differentiates us from individuals who are working-class or live in poverty (Faniko, Lorenzi-Cioldi, Ghisletta, Øyslebø, Sørensen, Shalsi, & Chipeaux, 2015). We justify our privileged positions by rationalizing "If I did it, others can do it as well." It is difficult to admit that our hard work has not been the only factor that allows us to own a home, for example. We remain reluctant to challenge systems of oppression and marginalization because, in different ways, they work for us. It has been easier to normalize segregation as long as we have our spot assured. Throughout this process of segregation, we contribute to repeating patterns of marginalization in which those with less income and opportunities continue to receive mediocre health-care services and inadequate education (Lipsitz, 2013). We certainly see the injustices out there, but only when they directly affect our pocketbooks, comfort, and peace of mind.

A common way to justify inequalities and remove ourselves from such problematic behaviors is by employing a meritocratic narrative. Adams (2013) refers to meritocracy as a principle that states that "hard work and talent will be rewarded" (p. 143). Said principle and the way we have been enacting it in Mexico, enforces the idea that poverty is a choice, which can be avoided, and that comes from laziness and a lack of effort. Meritocracy is rooted in the idea that everyone, regardless of their identities, financial status, and social context, has the same opportunities of being successful; those in disadvantaged conditions have not moved away from poverty because of their own choices (Franiko et al., 2015; Cech, 2017).

The concept of meritocracy sounds ideal for many of us because it eases our guilt and responsibility when we are held accountable for perpetuating marginalization. Meritocracy allows us to comfortably claim that we have earned what we have with no advantages whatsoever "fair and square." Meritocracy places the higher classes in a position of power, rightfulness, and moral superiority. Adhering to the principle of meritocracy would entail the justification of poverty, pinning the responsibility into the individuals who experience it, and excusing ourselves and the major power structures.

3   Documented in the United States

> ...the U.S. government has built a brutal system of immigration control and policing that criminalizes immigration status, normalizes the forcible separation of families, destabilizes communities and workplaces, and fuels widespread civil rights violations. This "immigration policing regime" is also fueling racial discrimination and hate against immigrants and those perceived to be foreign born or "illegal." (National Network for Immigrant and Refugee Rights, 2010, para. 5)

Alongside the United States-Mexico border, as documented immigrants with race, language and class privileges, a tourist and/or student visa, our discomforts to cross the border are minimal. For instances, we are bothered by menial inconveniences such as putting our paperwork together, paying for a visa application, attending the meetings and interviews to receive our documentation. If we count on such resources, it is very likely that crossing the border is a choice more than a need. We choose to get in long lines to cross the border, knowing that we will cross without further and expected *annoyances* such as questions from the United States border customs, car inspections, and sometimes rudeness and hostility at the checkpoints. Yet, we know that we will be allowed to cross, and have the liberty of coming back to our country of origin.

Such inconveniences cannot be compared with the struggles and endurance of undocumented immigrants who for years, have been abused both in Mexico and in the United States as they seek out asylum, safety, job opportunities and a better life. Being documented in the United States has allowed me to have peace of mind, it has allowed me safety. I did not earn my documentation by merit, I did not do anything extraordinary for the world in order to get my tourist visa; I only demonstrated income. Yet the narrative for undocumented immigrants on both sides of the border has been *privileges must be earned; you must work hard and prove that you are worthy of being in the United States.* News flash, I did not do anything other than existing with all the privileges that are given by my identities. Yet my race, education, English proficiency, positionality, and material possessions signified worthiness to the officer in control of my visa approval, to the system in general. Unlike the visas that are denied to low-income individuals and people of color on a continuous basis, mine was approved in a heartbeat. In general, all these elements that emerge from privilege, worked in my favor as they aligned with the strict and expensive requirements to cross the border.

The political climate during 2016 in the United States is a good example of our privilege as documented students in the US, and privileged documented Mexicans in general. During this time period, my friends and teachers kept asking me if I was safe. I appreciated their concerns with regard to my safety, but of course I was, and I am. I have both a student visa and a scholarship from my country. Even if, for any reason, the policy that protects my status was to be revoked, I can still rest assured that I have the option of going back to a country that has never turned its back to me. This is because none of my identities challenge the dominant norms. While I was appalled upon hearing the 45th US President's statements about Mexican people, both in Mexico and the US, xenophobia and racism have been consistently enacted towards people of color and undocumented immigrants, not White, privileged and documented Mexicans. For a moment, like many of my fellow documented, White/White-passing and privileged Mexicans, I felt such words as personal. I thought, "We are not the worst. We are students; therefore, we are worthy of being here in your country because we work hard and are worthy of a space." The 45's rhetoric is easy for us to challenge because he is seen as the biggest villain, and his opinions, in a way, make us feel less ugly, less racist, and less problematic. Though pointing out the flaws of a public figure who is being a bigot is important, this focus has conveniently kept us from looking within ourselves—kept us from identifying the ways in which we have been the same toward non-Mexican Latinxs, immigrants, asylum seekers, and people of color. In which ways have we perpetrated or allowed marginalization?

White Mexicans—particularly the ones who, like me—possess the privileges granted by tourist and/or student visas, for the very first time felt *personally* attacked. We felt as if 45's words were a potential danger to us. Our documented status does not challenge his views of immigrants. Instead, our documented status—the fact that we are students/tourists—reinforces his idea of what a good immigrant is and what we should look like. Though there's a chance of experiencing discrimination, rudeness, or discomfort as we speak our native language, our privileged identities seldom challenge racist individuals. This is especially the case when the color of our skin is white or close to white.

The results of the 2016 United States' election did not threaten my personal safety or permanence in this country. On top of my racial privileges, I have an i20 visa, a student visa, and, therefore, the respect of many racists and xenophobes. My documentation is not the only thing that protects me from discrimination and from deportation, my skin tone also protects me—even more so than the papers. Immigration and Customs Enforcement (ICE) agents are not harassing me or asking me for papers when we cross paths. My privilege as an international student has given me the certainty that my migratory status in this country is a choice, not a necessity, as it is for undocumented immigrants. I knew that 45's discourse of xenophobia and racism, even though directly addressed Mexico and Mexican people, do not have the same consequences for me as it does for undocumented People of Color in the US. 45 and his supporters are very unlikely to target me or someone who shares my privileges.

After his many hateful speeches aimed at the Mexican community, many of us felt personally attacked and let our hate flow throughout social media. What we did not do was acknowledge how his marginalizing speech also targeted populations that we have marginalized and segregated for a long time in our country, such as undocumented immigrants and asylum seekers from Central America. We've been acting as if the US president's words were a new type of attack, how he had the audacity of discriminating against us. However, we often fail to acknowledge the experiences of individuals who are actually at risk of losing everything they have, given the political climate and the societal power structures.

The US president's rhetoric conveniently filled our need to have a "bad guy" who was not *us*—the advantaged and non-vulnerable people from Mexico. Here we are, all fired up tweeting and posting how he cannot mess with *us*, claiming a sentiment of unity and appreciation towards the undocumented community in the United States. Yet we have failed to see the inconsistencies of such *unity*, which immediately disappears as we continue to attribute poverty to a lack of hard work and as we continue to judge Mexicans and undocumented immigrants from Central America for seeking survival in the United States. Such unity is erased every time we make or dismiss a comment that disempowers undocumented people, and when we use ourselves as examples of entitlement because we had the means to obtain legal documentation to go to the United States.

Not long ago, I was listening to a local Mexican radio station from Ciudad Juarez. The topic was undocumented immigration of Mexican citizens into US territory. The phone lines of the radio station were open for radio-listeners to call and speak their minds about the issue of undocumented immigrants, and the struggles they are having in the United States given Trump's rhetoric towards Mexican people. Of course, Central and Southern American countries were not addressed within this segment, because Mexican nationalism continues to be at the core of our narrative and discussions.

Throughout my 15-minute commute, the narratives against Trump focused solely on how he should acknowledge that "some of us do the right thing, work hard, save money, and earn our visas." I listened to at least five people who supported Trump's narrative, saying that those who crossed the border illegally had "wronged us all." Although some calls addressed the xenophobic content of Trump's speech, the language remained nationalistic and ethnocentric. People rarely acknowledged how Mexicans with visas were not as vulnerable as undocumented immigrants in the United States. Nobody addressed immigrants or asylum seekers from other countries, people from Central America, and other vulnerable populations that were targeted through the hateful rhetoric.

A mixture of nationalism, racism, xenophobia, classism, and the privilege given by anonymity allowed local radio-listeners to express their feelings with regard to undocumented immigrants. One of them argued: "They are not real Mexicans because they are running away from the problems." The statements revolved around nationalist catch phrases such as *"la Patria es primero,"* and how a "true Mexican" would never abandon their country. We learn from a very young age to be toxically patriotic—to see Mexico as the best and most important country in Latin America. We are taught biased history lessons in which white-looking mestizaje is perpetrated as an attempt to designate an identity that homogenizes us as a nation and that should make us proud (Ortiz & García, 2017; Yankelevich, 2017). Yet, these biased teachings in our early education should not bear the entire blame, nor should it be a shield to protect us from accountability.

The dialogue on the radio show broke down into *them* (undocumented, Indigenous, immigrants, refugees, poor, presumably not hard working enough) and *us* (documented, presumably hard-working, privileged). In this situation, according to narratives of people calling in to the radio show, *they/them* are the ones who could not stay because they were motivated by choice instead of need. *They/them* were the working-class and low-income Mexicans who "ran away from the problems," the ones who "should know better" about respecting the rules, and should settle for the lives they have been given, surrendering to poverty and working harder even though there are very few chances to improve their quality of life. On the other hand, *we/us* are the ones who "should be an example for them, as we play by the rules." Nonetheless, *we/us* certainly come from privileged positions; probably went to private schools; have access to wholesome nutrition; live in gated neighborhoods; and benefit from healthcare and/or can afford private medical expenses. We have all of the privileges that allow us to play by the rules, which we do because we can afford to do so.

I wish I could say I was surprised as I heard people's hateful comments. I also wish I could fully exclude myself from that reality, but writing about problematic folks does not redeem me from all of the times I heard xenophobic comments and did not stop them. There were also times that I assumed that I was better and more deserving of my privileges because I was *doing things right*. I made these assumptions instead of understanding how people have different needs than I do, how people with fewer privileges must focus on survival, and how sometimes that entails migrating to a different country without documents.

There were many times that I let my personal biases shape my perception of others and feel as if I was a *real* Mexican or *more* Mexican than others, and there were times that I let my own toxic nationalism shape my perception of others. Not being directly classist, racist or xenophobe through comments to others does not excuse me from being part of the problem. Although I never blatantly pointed out others' less privileged positionality, I let the nationalism shape my biases and understand *Mexicanidad* in a segregated way. Simply assuming that I was better, or a *good citizen* by following immigration rules, enforces the principles of meritocracy. Both individually and collectively this mindset is toxic and marginalizing, as it invalidates other people's experiences, and aims to erase all the advantages and privileges that a documented status involves.

As I was listening to the radio show, I was waiting to hear some accountability, but I knew it was not going to happen. I knew it because I was concomitantly reflecting on all the times in which I failed to acknowledge and challenge my own nationalism—what did/does it look like? As I listened to others speak from privileged positions, I could not stop thinking about the possible ways in which I had enacted xenophobia, classism and nationalism in the past.

It is very easy to take a side and portray oneself as the one who is *doing the right thing*, particularly when nationalist values are present in the conversation. Mexican nationalism encourages that; for years we have been following a pathway of a pride that puts all identities in the same box, claiming that race and ethnic diversity are almost non-existent in our country (Rico, 2016; Yankelevich, 2017). Such erasures include the endurances and struggles of vulnerable populations. Through a meritocratic lens, less advantaged populations are portrayed as non-deserving, lazy, not hard-working enough. We often fail to consider the different identities and experiences that impede underprivileged groups to grow financially in an inequitable country like Mexico. Even when they find ways of growing financially, perhaps by migrating to the United States seeking survival, different opportunities, and many other reasons that should not concern us, we find ways to belittle their efforts throughout mockery and rejection (Rico, 2016). We disown them as Mexicans for leaving a country that has only turned its back on them.

For a significant part of my life, I have been listening to narratives of dismissal aimed at Mexican Americans in the United States. Ever since I was in elementary school, English teachers repeated how "tacky and ugly" it was to mix English and Spanish, "we do not do that, it sounds ugly and it is incorrect." That narrative was usually accompanied by statements such as "the Chicanos speak like that," in a tone of mockery and disrespect, and as a rationale not to do it. Though it would be an easy escape, I will not blame my education for perpetrating or not stopping behaviors, actions, and discourse that segregate and discriminate.

To some extent, my schooling and education influenced my ideologies, but it has been my reluctance to engage in self-reflexivity that for years has soothed my conscience and allowed me to think that I was not part of this issue. It shouldn't have taken me so long to understand my ignorance and learn from it. This exemplifies how privileged I've been, that checking myself and exploring these issues have been a choice for me. I truly believed the Mexican nationalist, discriminatory and meritocratic narratives, internalized them, and failed to challenge them when I had the chance of doing so. The comfort of my positionality and my own toxic ideologies regarding meritocracy and *right* or *wrong* supported such a mindset. I could afford passing judgment upon others and remove myself from a problematic conversation as I pleased. Moreover, it is rather comfortable to identify ourselves as *the real hard workers*, the ones who have proudly earned every peso we have, and believe that we should not feel responsible for the endurance, struggles, and marginalization of other groups.

Accepting that we have been imposing obstacles to disadvantaged individuals on the basis of race, class, ethnicity, sexuality, religion, physical ability, migratory status, and many other identities is an unpopular challenge. Perhaps self-scrutiny and accountability threaten our comfortable positions of power, or maybe we never think of ourselves as contributors to inequities, negative portrayals, and erasure of vulnerable communities.

4   The Value of English

My parents' concept of growth and professional success was strongly connected to the ability to speak English. They understood English language proficiency as an important skill for survival in a competitive world. My mother is the fifth child of nine children in her family. They all received a public education in Mexico. They also moved a lot from one school to the next and she narrates being in crowded classrooms with the bare minimum of resources. My mother and her siblings would commute using public transportation and taking several buses on their own, in pairs, and in triads in order to protect the youngest. She says that in her commutes back home, she would see the children in the private schools, leaving at 2:00 pm. She remembers perceiving these children as happier than she and her siblings. She recalls their neat uniforms and their discipline as they lined up outside of school waiting for their parents to pick them up. My mom knew that all of these children would have an advantage over her and her siblings, as they had the ability to speak English. My mother thought that that was the best education a child could ever get, and she always wanted her children to attend one of those schools and receive what she thought was the best education.

Unlike my mother, my father comes from an upper-middle-class family. He attended private schools exclusively. Although his education was private, my father's education was not bilingual. This meant that his chances of specializing and going to graduate school abroad as, most of his colleagues did, were decreased. In spite of my father's ingrained machismo and expectations for us as women, he knew that job opportunities in Mexico were competitive. Therefore, he wanted to provide us with an education that would allow me and my sister to have more skills to navigate the world. Both of my parents were clear as to how "English was the universal language." They knew that English would allow us to move up in the Mexican socioeconomic ladder, as it did for those who were at the top.

My sister and I attended a private elementary school and got enrolled in a couple of English courses offered by a Community College in El Paso, Texas. Before the 9/11 attacks in the United States, it was easier and faster to cross the border with a tourist visa. Since we were only crossing to learn English, we did not need a student visa for that weekly commute. Our teachers only spoke to us in English and paid careful attention to our learning needs, as our parents were paying a fee and expected us to learn. Unlike most undocumented children and/or underprivileged Latinxs in the United States, my sister and I received a bilingual education that was friendly and adapted to our learning needs as English Language Learners. For us, English as a second language was not an imposed tool for survival, but an extra element to our already existing privileges.

Speaking English in Mexico, socially denotes a higher status in the socioeconomic ladder, therefore, it also suggests superiority over others who cannot speak it (Despagne, 2015). Our perception of English is not only influenced by our classist narrative, but also highly mirrors racist attitudes that are rooted in our ways of knowing and understanding the world. Furthermore, racist and xenophobic realities emerge when the ability to speak English is addressed. For instance, people in Mexico who can speak English *correctly* often make fun of those who cannot, calling them *nacos*—which is Spanish for tacky—or *indios*, referring to the Indigenous communities in Mexico in a derogatory manner. Presumably *good* English and Spanish are linked to class and scarcity of resources, in Mexico such elements are racialized. The term *indio* is commonly used towards people who mispronounce or misuse words in English; when individuals struggle with technology; and as a derogatory term in which White Mexicans refer to People of Color. When used this way, such a term implies inferiority, ignorance, and anti-Indigenous *ideology*.

Alongside other privileges, speaking English has allowed me to enroll in a university in the United States. If I did not have English proficiency, I would not have been an eligible candidate for the program I am studying. Therefore, I would not have the funding I received from the Mexican government. Most graduate programs in Mexico and around the world, demand a certain percentage of English proficiency (Valdés-Rodríguez, Palacios Wassenaar, & Sánchez-Cruz, 2017). As a result, academic growth, which highly influences one's position of power and income, depends on one's English proficiency. Reflecting on the significance of learning English under privileged conditions has helped me understand the opportunities it affords me, as well as to reflect upon the restrictions and barriers imposed on those whose experience with English is a violent imposition.

5   Classist Depictions of Underprivileged Populations

In Mexico, the middle and upper classes have mastered the art of reading people and make assumptions based on their income and material possessions. Having the latest technological devices, expensive automobiles, grade of education, and job positionality have become a means of earning respectability and superiority over other people. This is particularly the case among the upper classes.

In Ciudad Juarez, mockery toward production operators in *la maquiladora* [industry/factories] is a clear example of classist behavior. This phenomenon encompasses several forms of oppression that intertwine with classism. Ciudad Juarez has a large number of industries and factories owned by corporations from different parts of the world. These companies are looking for cheap labor. Therefore, they settled in Mexico, as well as other countries where there was access to cheap labor. For years, Ciudad Juarez has received migrants from different states of Mexico. The migrants come seeking to work in the maquiladoras and to establish themselves in the city. They do so to provide for their families and/or survive the poverty and shortages of opportunities that exist in their states. Production operators in the maquiladoras are those who occupy the lowest positions, receive the lowest salaries, and work the longest hours.

Through a bigoted narrative, the middle and upper classes in Ciudad Juarez depict the production operators of the maquiladora as unintelligent. The most recent form of mockery toward the workers of the maquiladora is through social media. Local pages in social networks are dedicated to the creation of local *memes*. Said imagery portrays those who work in the maquiladora as ignorant individuals who make *poor* financial choices with their salary, suggesting that this part of the population has chosen to struggle financially. They mock the workers' need for public transportation, their lack of access to the latest technology, their uniforms, the clubs and bars they go to, among other things. The creators of this content, in a condescending tone of contempt, depict women who work in la maquiladora as classless and if they are referring to women who have children, they often portray them as neglectful single mothers—a status which is highly shamed in Mexico as well (Valdez, 2018). Overall, these depictions state that those who work in the *maquila* are never going to get out of poverty and imply that it is appropriate to use their lives and experiences as a comedic opportunity. The creators of these platforms are not alone. There are thousands of people, particularly locals, who enjoy and share the content. In this way, they are demonstrating a position of approval—signifying that they share those ideas which amuse them—the grueling working hours and the inferior socioeconomic level of others.

Classism is not only one of the predominant forms of oppression in Mexico, it is also one of the most exploited issues in the media industry. One of the most basic examples are *telenovelas* [soap operas]. Most of these national dramas portray the experiences and endurances of rich White Mexicans who end up falling in love with fellow White or white-passing working-class characters. The stories are usually similar; they are bad-quality productions of rich people involved in love triangles or going through existential crises. Whichever the case, the rich family always has servants comprised of Indigenous people, People of Color, and people who live in marginalized areas of Mexico. These depictions reinforce many problematic issues in Mexico; such as racism, sexism and classism. The soap operas teach the audience that the experiences that are important are those lived by the White and wealthy people of Mexico. In soap operas, poverty is portrayed as a sad but inevitable reality, and the only way out is marriage and/or compassion from the upper classes. In soap operas, the opportunities for the lower class to progress are one hundred percent in the hands of wealthy families and depend upon their compassion or attention to the lower classes. The media and entertainment industry in Mexico has created an empire based on socioeconomic difficulties and injustices, by portraying powerless communities and individuals at the mercy of the charity, help, and good heartedness of those who are more privileged.

Othering has a connotation of excluding a person from a group to highlight income, ethnic, and religious differences as well as physical abilities, for example. "For people who are stigmatized as inferior, the formation of the "Other" takes shape in ways of marginalization and alienation" (Labrie, 2018, p. 33). Othering can happen in many ways, such as making verbal statements that separate us from an individual or a certain group of people, as well as denying resources and services to individuals based on their identities. The intersection between class and education in my life allowed me to experience, learn and even enact the phenomenon of othering in many ways. Though I do not recall anyone literally telling us at school that we were better than children in poverty, statements of othering were made on a continuous basis.

As a consequence for failing to solve a math problem, messing up our homework, or not wearing our uniform according to the rules, we would hear threats such as: "Since you are not good at school, I guess you are going to end up selling chewing gum in the street like poor children do." Statements such as this are rooted in three classist ideologies. The first one I can identify is the association of school incompetence with poverty.

My schooling shaped my inconsistent understandings and perceptions of poverty. I internalized these understandings until I grew up and learned the importance of challenging my own values, and beliefs. Poverty was oftentimes used as a slur. My teacher used concepts related to poverty as a slur in several ways. For instance, he would position *us*—students in his class—above poor children. He would imply that we were better and that we needed to act accordingly. The classist message behind his words warned us to be careful not to fall into poverty by engaging in patterns of laziness. Secondly, his use of such rhetoric erased the painful and abusive experiences of kids subjugated to child labor, carelessly highlighting the circumstances of poor children and their families as examples of lack of motivation or failure. Third, my teacher presumed that belonging and succeeding in a private school environment would guarantee safety from poverty and would assure our permanence on the socioeconomic ladder. In my school, and throughout different spaces I've occupied, poverty has been discussed and understood as a consequence of not working hard enough, or not being smart enough. *Nos lavamos las manos*, we blame the victim.

CHAPTER 2

A Catholicism I Know

This chapter addresses some of the intersections between the Catholic religion and other identities, such as sexuality, race, and class. I intend to provide a portrayal of how Catholic religion in Mexico aids in the ongoing marginalization of certain groups in this country. Moreover, drawing from my personal experiences with religion, I discuss how Catholics in Mexico, who are the vast majority of the population (Coss, Coss, & Parra, 2018), have learned, internalized and perpetuated discriminatory behaviors towards minority and vulnerable groups. My intention is not to disrespect those whose beliefs are rooted within the Catholic church, but to share my own experiences with this religion as I discuss issues of power abuse, marginalization, and accountability. I see it as pertinent to this narrative, to deconstruct some of the messages I received throughout my years in Catholic schools. This is especially significant given how those messages later influenced my self-perception and my understanding of the world. During my childhood, because I attended a Catholic elementary school, I learned and believed many concepts and ideas of this religion to the core.

1   Class and Catholic-isms

The different schools and Catholic environments that I have been a part of perpetrated benevolent classism, in which we all became part of a problematic dynamic of *charitable work*. I would constantly hear how grateful I needed to be to God, as he loved me so much that I had the opportunity to eat, dress, have a family and a home, unlike children in Africa who were dying of starvation. Within this rhetoric, we learned that God favored us for being his faithful followers and being a part of the Catholic community. We also learned that it was our moral duty to help others by giving them some of our resources and *helping* them find Jesus in their hearts. Every winter was time to donate to people who lived in poverty in Ciudad Juarez. This event was marked in the school's agenda—once a year we got to be helpful humans who saved someone else's Christmas. The narrative in which we were *helping* placed us immediately in a position of power, in which we were choosing to "share our wealth" with those who were "less fortunate and blessed than us." Because of the privileges that my identity granted me and because of the lack of consciousness that I had regarding the different forms of oppression, I became numb, and I normalized poverty.

We like our meritocratic narrative because it makes us look and feel good—proud of ourselves, even more so when we have God's blessing. Within the spaces I occupied, the Catholic Church never challenged the systems of oppression. Local priests in Juarez would have us pray for the poor and less-fortunate during mass, as they also prayed for our governors and policymakers, asking God to illuminate their minds and have them act the rightful way. Although the Mexican government emancipated from religion in the middle of the 20th century (Blancarte, 2008), the Catholic church has historically had a strong interference in its government affairs, strongly supporting conservative policy-making, as long as it aligns with the principles of Catholicism (Gómez-Peralta, 2007).

Priests would not hesitate to let us know their political views and how they felt regarding controversial issues such as abortion and birth control. Moreover, local religious leaders have often mentioned how people who live in poverty are happier as they have more children: *"son pobres de dinero pero ricos en amor"* [they are poor in income but rich with love]. Historically, this religion has conquered the Indigenous peoples all over the world. Let's not forget that Catholicism was imposed on Indigenous people by the Spanish colonizers, now the affluent and White-passing Mexicans, who claim and have closer connection to Spain, continue the colonization, now through discrimination (Grinde, 2004). Not only have priests disempowered vulnerable communities throughout disempowering narratives, the Catholicism I know has used its platform as a performative space in which we selectively *share* our resources, but each socioeconomic group stays in their place. We do not make a lot of noise regarding injustices, poverty, or femicide. We pray a lot, though. We pray because thoughts and prayers do not challenge or transgress the oppressor. Praying can be done in the comfort of our homes; through prayer we never put ourselves in the spotlight. As we learned in school and catechism, we stay seated and in silence—looking from a distance.

2   Diversity?

According to González and Ríos (2017), Catholicism in Mexico is not a hegemonic religion, as it used to be decades ago. In fact, it has lost several followers who are now affiliating with other Christian religions. Kan (2014) highlights how the Catholic hegemony in Mexico decreased significantly in the 1980's. Yet, Catholicism continues to be the most practiced religion in Mexico

(Coss, Coss, & Parra, 2018; de la Torre, 2018); it is the most validated and represented religion portrayed by the media. Furthermore, although I am currently disengaged from Catholicism, I am familiar with the traditions, values, and practices of the religion. Therefore, I am aware of the privileges I am afforded solely for knowing the language and practices, having positive representation in the media. As a group, Catholics in Mexico can be a hostile group, especially to individuals who practice different religions.

After the Mexican independence, a struggle between the Catholic church and the Mexican state began. At the beginning of the 20th century and after the Cristero War in Mexico, the Catholic church negotiated its power with the Mexican government. In paper, the church stepped away from political decisions and public education (Castillo, 2014). Yet, it continues to educate individuals from kindergarten to the university level through the private sector. In Mexico, being affiliated with a religion other than Catholicism is quite a challenge. Even though there are a variety of religions practiced in Mexico, they are often erased and invalidated. This is because part of the Mexican identity that we continue to claim as valid revolves around the principles of Catholicism (de la Torre, 2016).

The narrative I remember within Catholicism in Mexico constantly drilled on principles of superiority, particularly superiority over other religions. Our catechism teachers taught us not to open the doors of our homes to people who had other ideologies, as "they were inferior, ignorant, and had bad intentions." We should only open the door if we had our dogma ready. To do so, we were expected to: "Read the bible and know your passages" and "Be prepared to defend your religion, your God." It was as if we were in charge of educating them with what we thought was the absolute and universal truth. We learned some things about other religions, but not in a culturally responsive manner. Instead, we went over other religions through a sort of *fun-fact* type of narrative, most of the time in a diminishing way.

The rhetoric used toward religious diversity was disrespectful and diminished the experience of Jehovah's Witnesses, Buddhists, Muslims, Christians, Protestants, and pretty much every other religion. The catechism teachers and priests would preach to us about how all these *other* people were *motherless*, as they did not believe in the Virgin Mary and her manifestations of miracles in the same way Catholics do. Teachers didn't label these behaviors as discriminatory or deeply disrespectful. Instead, these marginalizing thoughts were taught as a being "Christ's soldiers." The core message was: "God approves! We are defending his church as an institution that holds the universal truth, the only religion to respect and acknowledge."

That being said, discrimination towards other religions should not be attributed solely to a traditional religious schooling, but also to the lack of accountability that comes with being in a comfortable position of privilege and presumed rightfulness. It is my choice and responsibility to acknowledge the toxicity of unchallenged problematic ideologies. I have never been an enthusiast of Catholicism; yet as a young girl and teenager, I always occupied spaces that were Catholic-centered. Because my parents were raised Catholic, they wanted to pass on the tradition and values of the Catholic church to my sister and me. My mother says she always felt as though religion was the healthiest and most appropriate values to raise and educate her children.

I never felt the need to go to church to have peace of mind, and I was definitely not interested in studying the bible in order to argue with people who practiced other religions. And I wasn't convinced that having good comebacks for the Jehovah's Witnesses was enough of a reason to pay attention in mass. Nonetheless, I cannot deny that I did internalize many of these ideologies of judgment and division. Being part of the majority group makes it very easy for a person to not worry about the *others* who, according to your religion, are doing things wrong and are probably condemned to hell. I was in a comfortable place, so why challenge myself and the ideologies that have shaped my formal education? I did not see them as problematic, rather I was bored by them. Back then, I could not articulate the issues in which the church was being problematic, as I was not directly affected by such principles.

I have been privileged as I fit in these dominant environments in Mexico, even though I do not choose to be a part of them. As most Catholics in Mexico, I have never been discriminated against for my religious affiliations the same way many Jehovah's Witnesses, Muslims, Buddhists, and other individuals in Mexico have. Knowing the language of Catholicism, attending to the dominant rituals, and being immersed in that environment for so long gave me a sense of belonging, and I benefitted from being part of the majority (Schlosser, 2003). I was never the child who everyone judged or questioned for not celebrating Christmas. I was never shamed for not believing in Virgin Mary. Even if I did not like the rituals, ceremonies, and religious messages, I was and am still part of that great majority, because I have the literacy and comprehension of rituals, language, and behaviors. I also reinforce colonizing messages of segregation—messages that, in spite of my separation from the Catholic church, emerge sporadically. These messages convey that *we are right, everybody else is wrong, and here's why...*

3   Our Bigotry towards LGBTQ+ Groups

Individuals who do not align with heteronormativity pertain to the most discriminated groups in Catholic environments. Although this is not my experience, I have experienced mass, and as I mentioned before, I have received an education based on traditional and conservative values that marginalize LGBTQ+ groups. Several homilies, which are the lectures during the Catholic mass ceremony, address the familial values that the Catholic church supports. These families are binary, patriarchal and heteronormative. The narrative of God creating a man and a woman with the purpose of them being together to create a family excludes, shames, and erases the experiences of individuals who are not heterosexual, non-binary, non-comforming, transgender, single parents raising children. I've heard priests say that God condemns homosexuality and that "non-binary gender identities are an ideology that needs to be eradicated."

Although unmarried couples and cisgender single parents (specially mothers) are constantly frowned upon, they do not endure discrimination and marginalization in the same way as LGBTQ+ individuals. Such groups are not even considered a part of the Catholic communities in Mexico unless they express their desire to change "their ways." The only way to be welcomed or embraced into the community is if there are demonstrations of repentance and willingness to change through the use of conversion therapy and other painful and procedures that claim to effectively repress and *correct* a sexual orientation that the church considers unacceptable.

Catholic religion is one of the first environments in which we learn how to "other." The outlier or the *other*, is that individual who, because of their sexual orientation or gender, has challenged the cut-through binary norms of gender and sexuality that Mexican society expects (Bernal, 2018). The *other* is oftentimes portrayed as problematic and in need of being *fixed*. The Catholic community is seldom discouraged from discriminating the LGBTQ+ (Lesbian, Gay, Bisexual, Transgender, Queer, Intersex, Asexual) community. On the contrary, the priests often encourages their congregation to show *them* the "good way of God," and dissociate from them if they refuse to change who they are. Consequently, those the Catholic church considers outliers cannot expect the community to embrace and include them as they are. As Catholics, we learn that this is what needs to happen to non-heterosexual people, therefore, the community collectively rejects them.

The danger here is that this religious community continues to be the predominant one in Mexico, perpetrating aggressions and marginalization of people who do not fit the cookie cutter image of goodness. Thus, aggression and intolerance toward diversity are oftentimes passive-aggressive and disguised with a narrative of concern for the spiritual wellbeing of God's children. The Catholic church I know has a narrative of *acceptance* that comes from a supposed place of loving the outliers in spite of the *sinner's perversions. La culpa* inserts itself at all times in Catholic rhetoric, even more so within narratives of alleged acceptance. *La culpa* threatens folks through reminders of how your actions and identities might be wronging God. Judgment and rejection are disguised as support and solidarity, as if saying "I welcome you but you must change who you are."

Heterosexuality identities are central elements in the discussion of privilege. This is particularly true in a country like Mexico, where machismo and Catholicism are central when it comes to defining standards and expectations. My identity as a cisgender heterosexual woman did not and does not challenge the norms. I have not had individuals scrutinizing my image, partners, sex life, or sexual orientation. "Cisgender people are those whose gender identity, role, or expression is considered to match their assigned gender by societal standards" (Taylor, 2013, p. 455). As an outsider, and someone who belongs to a majoritarian oppressive group, it is not my place to define the endurances of the LGBTQIA community. However, discussing how the heterosexual Catholic community in Mexico has contributed to different forms of oppression towards the non-gender binary and non-heterosexual individuals is both appropriate and necessary.

Gay marriage has been allowed in a few states in Mexico since 2006. Ten years later, the Federal government proposed the unification of this law in the whole country, and the Mexican congress rejected such proposal. Ever since 2006, and the idea of legally validating same sex marriage, there has been a backlash from conservative groups in Mexico. An example of such groups is *"Frente Nacional por la Familia,"* a Catholic group that, in the name of the traditional family (father, mother, and as many children as god sends your way) opposes gay marriage, divorce, abortion, and homoparental adoption to name a few. Heterosexual people have not ceased to express unsolicited opinions regarding rights for the LGBTQ+ community, with a common response being; "I respect it [homosexuality, queerness, transgender, non-binary or non-conforming identities], but I do not want it in my home." Family members, friends, teachers, neighbors and people around me have made this statement, which is a disclaimer—an attempt to not be the villain. At the same time, statements such as this exclude certain groups of people and allow us to use the power that heterosexuality gives us to determine what is valid. Our society is very permissive with heterosexual people, it allows us to experience a sense of superiority and entitlement. LGBTQ+ people continue to be a vulnerable population in Mexico, as our bigotry keeps pushing them to the margins, fostering unsafe environments throughout different spaces.

I am not personally harmed by the societal disapproval that comes with identifying as other than cisgender/heterosexual in Mexico. Heterosexual people in Mexico do not endure the same challenges, because our humanity and identities are not questioned. It is safe for us to exist in most spaces, particularly when seeking spirituality. However, we do love to have opinions and question and discuss everyone else's sexual orientations and gender identities. The overwhelming approval of our heterosexual ways of living and the allowed discrimination of *others* in our religious spaces makes us feel entitled to interfere, have opinions, and let the world know that "we disagree" with homosexuality and gender diversity. We also feel entitled to comment on how *it is ok for people to live their lives, but...* (insert discriminatory and religious centered statement here). This is what we do to the LGBTQIA community on a daily basis. We perpetuate and replicate, at the micro and macro levels, different forms of oppression in which we impose barriers that prevent access to the resources that we have claimed as ours—privileges that we enjoy and take for granted.

The Catholic church in Mexico, as well as other predominant Christian religions, often addresses homosexuality as a sinful mental disorder (de la Torre, 2018), which is said to be a product of liberalism. Local priests in Ciudad Juarez have often claimed that the LGBTQ+ community is increasing because "we are living in times of debauchery," and that homosexual and transgender people had "chosen to live away from God." Attending mass ceremonies, and normalizing everything is said, is not an excuse for our failure as a community to challenge such a narrative. The heterosexual Catholic members, a majoritarian and powerful population in Mexico, has done a poor job challenging the significant and intentionally discriminatory rhetoric of our religion. For the heterosexual community, it is easier to accept the idea that gay, non-binary gender, and transgender individuals are in the wrong, because that makes us feel morally superior, with a sense of authority and entitlement to decide which ways of existing are appropriate (Lozano-Verduzco, 2017).

In Mexico, coworkers and figures in power constantly perpetuate homophobia towards their LGBTQ coworkers or subordinates by making inappropriate jokes (Boivin, 2014). A sense of safety due to multiple privileged identities, such as belonging to the Catholic religion enables such mockery and it protects it. After all, we are taught that homosexuality is a choice—a wrong one. Would things change if we did a better job questioning the messages behind the hour-long lectures given at church? What would happen if we dared to listen closely and pay attention to the signs of violence and marginalization that are voiced towards the LGBTQ community?

It is true that religious leaders are highly respected and hierarchically above the congregation members. As members or once-members of such communities, we are responsible to hold them accountable for their problematic behaviors and narratives. Instead of doing so, we continue accepting and perpetrating such rhetoric because it puts us in a place of superiority and rightfulness. In the end, we are as responsible as this institution and its problematic leaders for the high rates of discrimination towards gender and sexual orientation diversity in Mexico. The fact is that we refuse to look within and challenge ideas that seem beneficial for us and our humanity because our integrity, humanity, and dignity are not questioned.

Further, Mexican mainstream media openly mocks safe spaces for the LGBTQ+ community and the use of non-binary language. Our safety, and disregard for others' safety allows many of us to speak thoughtlessly, without any negative consequences. Rarely will a person be called out on their homophobia, particularly if it is disguised as a joke. Most of the confrontations I have had with homophobic family members and acquaintances end up with them stating that I cannot take a joke or do not have a sense of humor. Yet, demanding for accountability is necessary, even when bigotry is disguised as "harmless humor." It is in such moments when we should make each other uncomfortable and discuss the intentions and origins of hatred narrative.

Religion, education, family values, and mainstream media have fostered a sense of entitlement over other people's lives, behaviors, sexual orientations, and identities. Barriers and marginalization will prevail as long as we continue engaging in claims such as "I do not have anything against gay people, but..." This narrative is used by politicians to avoid the development of socially just laws that takes into consideration the rights of LGBTI+ people, but our ongoing reluctance to check and share our privileges is doing damage as well. "I do not have anything against gay people but..." is marginalizing and patronizing. It does not make us diverse, inclusive, progressive, or modern. It is imperative for us to begin checking ourselves and to begin questioning our privileges and the ways in which we have been using them. How am I perpetrating segregation? Am I calling out homophobia? Am I even able to recognize my own homophobic, machista and gender-binary prejudices? Does Catholicism (or whichever religion you practice) condone such forms of discrimination? What are the values and lessons do I need to unlearn in order to stop contributing to these forms of bigotry?

4   *Temor de Dios*: The Fear of God

A Catholic education has contributed to how I constructed my moral framework, my definitions of what is right and wrong for most of my childhood and adolescence. Such a framework bore a certain level of toxicity. I cannot attribute this solely to religion. I also contribute to the lack of accountability that is possible when one had a multi-leveled position of privilege. The Catholicism

I experienced and describe was centered in middle-class environments. The audience were working and middle-class people who were not on the margins of poverty. We were not attending church because we needed shelter, but because we thought it was the *right* thing to do–not only spiritually, but also morally.

Regardless of my lack of engagement with and motivation toward religion, the fear of God accompanied me throughout my childhood. The rigidness of a traditional Catholic school entailed disciplinary measures aligned with respect towards God and Jesus Christ. Throughout elementary school, we were often encouraged to look at an image of Jesus nailed to the cross and bleeding from his wounds because of our sins. The curriculum followed the government guidelines, and the pedagogy was not engaging for students. For the most part, we would read, copy texts to our notebooks, and be expected to understand mathematics from an explanation on the chalkboard. Yet, we were frequently encouraged to pray before starting a day in school, in order to achieve better scores and learning experiences; pedagogy and learning was mostly in God's hands.

The classroom management strategies followed along the same lines. For instance, being loud meant we were disrespecting God and making him (because God is male) angry. Our routines revolved around prayers, monthly masses, and discipline. Teachers and staff would constantly threaten us with the ideas of sin, punishment, and how easy it would be for us to go to hell if we did not behave, pray and adhered to the norms and principles of the Catholic church. We prayed before going to class, then the Angelus (a prayer that reminds us of Angel Gabriel announcing the Holy Conception to virgin Mary, reinforcing the greatness and holiness of purity and virginity) at 12:00 noon, and then a couple of prayers before heading home. Not learning our prayers by memory was one of the measures by which we were judged to be bad Catholics.

As most Catholics do, I got enrolled in a course in which I needed to be prepared to receive the Holy Communion. The first holy communion ceremony represents our readiness to take Jesus Christ's body, which is presented to us in the shape of sacramental bread, a thin piece of bread a little bit larger than a quarter coin. In order to take this step in Catholicism, children and adults must prepare. To do this, they become immersed in biblical passages, memorize prayers, learn how to pray the rosary, and enter the confessional for the first time to tell their sins to a priest. We are supposed to learn all these things and be ready to make a religious routine out of these lessons, as that would mean living a life under the guidelines of the church and God. Praying, going to church, confessing our sins, and then making reparations by praying as the priest commands would be the most important steps to be within the parameters of an acceptable Catholic person. Of course, this narrative is not as plainly described by catechism teachers. They go above and beyond to teach us how this sacrament is more than a symbol, but a commitment to our faith and a reinforcement of our identity as God's children.

The first holy communion is the first time in which Catholics are fed the body and blood of Jesus Christ. These elements, according to the Catholic church, are present in the bread and wine. The first holy communion is one of the seven sacraments—also known as the must-do-steps—in order to live a Catholic life *by the book*. This sacrament requires people, usually children, to attend a workshop to learn the main values of the Catholic church: the prayers, the rosary, and different symbols that are important in our religion. This step also means that we get to achieve the final goal of our preparation: to receive the Eucharist. Part of such preparations requires Catholics to confess our sins to a priest, and afterward pray with remorse, as prescribed, in order to be forgiven. To prepare for my first holy communion at age eight, I learned some of the symbols; memorized the prayers, rituals, values, and traditions in the Catholic church; and I was also taught about the fear of God as a Catholic core value.

Our teachers told us that God is merciful and forgiving. Yet, they emphasized that we always need to remember our place of imperfection, vulnerability, and potential sinfulness. I am aware that some Catholic schools are more relaxed than others and that there are definitely stricter Catholic schooling methods in Mexico than what I experienced. However, my perception of religion and Catholic schooling were mostly fear-centered. I was afraid of upsetting God, making him angry, and of course, going to hell. We learned about "The fear of the Lord" as a core value of religion. We were supposed to feel protected by a God who was watching us at all times; God forgave our mistakes, but always surveilled.

Pope Francis, the current leader of the Catholic church, recently gave a statement regarding the fear of the Lord stating that this fear "is no servile fear, but rather a joyful awareness of God's grandeur and a grateful realization that only in him do our hearts find true peace" (Harris, 2014, para. 6). I surely didn't internalize fear of God as a safety net, or as an assurance of someone taking care of me and protecting me from danger. Most of my catechism and religion teachers were senior women with very traditional viewpoints on religion. They were single 60–70-year-old women, they were not nuns but dedicated their lives to God as they oftentimes said. Their backgrounds were rooted in conservative ideologies of Catholicism, which involved utilizing a lot of fear in order to convey guilt.

Constant reminders of the surveillance of God were accompanied by consequences related to hell and the devil, who had many names: *Lucifer, Satanás, El Diablo, El Demonio*, to name some. The journey through the first holy communion was not only rooted in having us learn prayers—though it seemed as if that was the only thing we did during the workshops. Our catechism teacher was so descriptive of Satan throughout her stories that it seemed as if she knew him personally, which made her a scary person to be around. She would tell us about his scarlet skin filled with boils and blisters because, of course, he inhabited the earth underground, where there is fire, eternal pain, and misery. I do not remember her addressing metaphor at all, so I took everything she said literally. We learned, through imagery and narrative, how the devil had huge horns, a terrifying look, and the power to manifest himself at any point and anywhere. Also, this teacher narrated the details of the labyrinths, corners, and alleys of hell with such confidence that it felt as if she was describing her own living room. My catechism teacher's story was always followed by how important it was for us to confess our sins to a priest. After all, if we did it right, God would forgive and love us despite our failings. All we needed was to confess and follow through our prayer prescription–of course feeling the repentance in our hearts.

I was fearful of doing things that disappointed God and getting myself a ticket to hell, so I tried make up for all the bad things I had done. Before the first holy communion ceremony, our school organized a trip to a church nearby. There, we would have a retreat—a day away from the school dedicated to church-centered activities in a Catholic temple. Furthermore, this religious retreat included meeting a priest for confession for the very first time. Our catechism teacher rode the bus with us. As always, she was addressing the disciplinary issues, telling us the usual things about being quiet and not to be disruptive because we were going to visit God's home. Before the bus driver even turned on the engine, she took a moment to have us reflect upon our sins. She said, "If you do not confess everything you did wrong—every sin, it does not matter how little–the sacramental bread will burn your throat once you eat it in the ceremony." My then fragile mind absorbed this narrative, which deprived my mother of many nights of sleep for the weeks to come. I would wake her up in the middle of the night panicking, thinking about all the religious threats that involved not confessing all my sins. I legitimately thought this would happen. What if I had done something very bad or offended God, but I could not remember at that moment? Was my throat going to be burned? I too was concerned about the possibility of Satan paying us a visit at night and taking us on a tour through hell. As the teacher said, he could drop by and invite us to commit sins at any moment. She did not bother to clarify to a group of third graders that it was a metaphor.

Though Catholic private education works well for some people, allowing them to experience and reinforce their faith in God, Catholicism can also represent an oppressive, censoring, and limiting force. In my case, this schooling system shaped and fed most of my fears related to sexuality. Additionally, it also informed the way I used to perceive and judge other women, LGBTI+ groups, Indigenous people, people from different religions, and other groups. My younger self would believe anything, anything taught in school and religious environments. It was not until I developed critical thinking and I matured that I became willing to explore and critique the formation of my ideologies and ways of thinking.

5 *Dios Me Ve*

To the naked eye, my elementary school was not a scary place. You could see children running around freely during recess and going to class. We wore our backpacks on our backs, of course. The kind with wheels were too disruptive according to the school administration. We had swing sets and a soccer court and spent our recess walking through a pathway made of old tires painted in different colors. However, the school's rigid Catholic values, rooted mostly in discipline and fear, were displayed in writing across some of the walls of several buildings.

All the restrooms inside and outside our classrooms had peculiar words all over the walls. The restroom stalls were very small and white, the lights were neon and when we turned them on we could see the white walls even brighter. Against such bright canvas, a message in bold letters popped out immediately. Written with black bold capital letters "DIOS ME VE," [God sees me]. This message was basically a warning of surveillance; that is how I interpreted it. I cannot recall anyone explaining clearly the intention of the message. I was not sure why I needed to be reminded that God was looking at me as I went to the bathroom. The sense of safety and privacy did not really exist in those little stalls. Reading this message as we pulled our pants down to go to the bathroom was scary and disturbing, not only because of the content of those three words but because of the fear I had towards God. I tried to go as fast as I could and get out before something scary would happen or before I could offend God in some way. Somehow my nakedness when removing my pants or skirt and releasing my body was a very bad thing and needed to be done quickly. Everything associated with nakedness and genitalia was forbidden and frowned upon.

I was fearful of God since I learned how to read. More than faith, love or devotion, I developed a deep respect towards God based on fear. The messages in the restroom not only reinforced the negativity of nakedness, they also made us aware of how God was looking at us at all times. This meant that privacy and intimacy were not real, and that we needed to be mindful of our bodies and actions. We needed to refrain from any behavior that would anger God. Throughout catechism classes and the ongoing discourse at church, we learned how women had the obligation to cover their bodies to respect God inside and outside of the church. Dressing provocatively invites men, "even the good ones," to commit sinful acts with and towards women. These acts included catcalling, rape, unfaithfulness, and any type of gender-based aggression. All of these lessons and ideologies merged together and translated to a fear of anything associated with sexuality and a profound shame of nakedness.

6   Between Silence and Sexuality

Please beware that this section includes content that addresses harassment and non-consensual touching.

After my first holy communion, I did not go into the confessional as often as mandated. I never felt the guilt or urge to go and tell my sins to a priest. When I was around 10 years old, I went to visit some family. They went to mass and confession on a weekly basis, so visiting them on a weekend entailed going to church with them. We all went to mass and then got in line to confess. I did not really want to do it, but I was already there. I thought, "why not?" The confessional was behind the church altar, and people would wait sitting on the wooden benches for their turn. The pathway toward the confessional was dark, but everyone seemed to know where to go, so I just followed. My cousin went in first and I paid close attention as I saw her leave the bench. I was not nervous; at that point I only saw confession as a pass to receive the holy communion like the grown-ups did. My cousin finished her confession in minutes and I was up next. I walked towards the confessional through the dark pathway. I was a little bit lost, as I had never been to confession in that church.

I finally arrived in the confessional. It looked like a rectangular box divided into two sections. The left side door was open, and it had a small piece of wood for me to sit down. I could not see the person behind the division, but I could hear his voice. I knew he was the priest that I saw and heard during mass. When I prepared for my holy communion, they taught us how to reflect on our actions moments before confession. I remembered that as I was waiting for my turn, and I already had my speech prepared. I was going to share with the priest how I had fights with my little sister often, or how angry I would get with my mother when she reminded me of my chores and responsibilities. I would probably mention too that I had very bad grades, and I felt guilty about spacing out in school. It is important to mention that I did not look or sound like a teenager, much less like an adult.

"*Ave Maria purísima*," said the priest. "*Sin pecado concebida*" I responded as I learned in school. The priest asked how long it had been since my last confession. "A month," I told him. I lied because I could not even remember. His next question was "Have you ever had impure thoughts?" I hesitated to respond right away, because I thought I was going to be the one doing the talking, instead of responding "yes or no" questions. "But I haven't done this in a long time," I thought. I remained quiet for a while and asked the priest what he meant by that. "Sexual thoughts," he replied. The room was dark, and I could only see the lights from the hallway outside. Even though I saw his face during mass, it felt as if the anonymity was his privilege instead of mine. Not being able to see the face of the person who asks you about sexual thoughts is frightening, even more so when it occurs in the dark. "No!" I said, almost in a defensive tone. Then he asked me if I ever lied; I said "yes." Asking whether I lied right after I said I did not experience sexual thoughts gave me the idea that he did not believe what I said. At that point I was not thinking about my sins and regret, I forgot my speech and what I had prepared. I felt embarrassed and could not stop thinking about the meaning of his first question. He did not seem too motivated in giving me life advice, guidance, or letting me know that it was okay to make mistakes and then reconsider my actions—all those things that I was told to expect after a confession. He seemed disappointed by the fact that I did not engage with his question about sexual thoughts. After obtaining the boring information about my sins, he told me to pray five Rosaries and 10 "Our Father" prayers. I went outside immediately after that, feeling uncomfortable and guilty.

I did not experience the promised feelings of peace and serenity that night. I remember overthinking my non-existing sexual thoughts. Was I lying? Maybe. I've thought about sex before—that was not an okay thing to do. I wondered about the priest's urge to know my thoughts and his interest to know about them before anything else. If what I had learned in catechism was correct, a confessional is where you go and debrief all your impure and sinful actions. Thinking about sexuality should definitely be a very bad thing then, something to be embarrassed about, something that a priest, who has "a direct link with God" needs to know about in order for me to be forgiven and not go to hell.

I started having a new understanding that everything related to sex was wrong and dirty and that it offended God.

My head was filled with questions regarding sexual thoughts and actions and the negative associations with them. These topics were not discussed with my parents. Though my mother always claimed to be open to answering questions, the concept of sexuality was too much of a taboo. I was learning in school how sex was a forbidden topic and something that we should not know until we were in high school. I did not want to learn; I really thought it was a dangerous and negative topic. Both in school and in family environments that I occupied, sexuality was addressed with code words or disguised as jokes that were too complicated for me to understand. Sexual acts, thoughts, and conversation were offensive to God. Thus, I did not want to have a conversation with my mother and open a can of worms. Perhaps, I thought, talking about sex would only unleash those thoughts that the priest referred to through his question. I internalized the idea that sexuality was a negative issue, and I did not want any information about it. The less I knew, the better I was. I felt the need to keep it to myself, as it was somehow embarrassing.

Throughout a conservative Catholic education, girls were constantly reminded of the importance of our purity and virginity as two of the main values of our womanhood. We were often threatened with comments such as, "A man will know if you're not a virgin." It was as if the condition of our tissue would automatically lessen our value as women. It was as if the only thing we should aspire to do was to become someone's wife. Our virginity was a gift for men—the ones who would give up on the adventures of life to establish a family and provide for us. We were encouraged to follow Virgin Mary's steps so that we could be good women and live in sanctity until we married some guy to whom we must devote ourselves. Such rhetoric included a lot of discussion of *decency*, dressing properly, and not showing a lot of skin so that we would not invite impure acts. Therefore, we would not bring rape and abuse upon ourselves, that is, women are blamed for the abuse they endure, not patriarchy, nor harmful men.

Further silences. I was around 12 years old when we went on a family road trip to California. My parents had been saving for a long time so that we could go to visit a theme park and get to know a little bit of Los Angeles. Eating in the theme park was out of our budget, so we would look for fast food or cheap places to eat. We decided to try a Chinese buffet place that was near to our hotel. My parents were the first ones in the line; my little sister and I were behind them. I grabbed my plate and kept walking with the line, looking at the food, and trying to decide what to eat. Suddenly I felt someone grab me from behind. It did not feel like an accident, or like when you bump into something. I froze. I even thought I bumped into something or that I had walked backward into a chair; I did not want to believe it was a hand. I was shaking and turned around. I saw a very tall man with white hair staring at me. He was making a strange gesture, as if he was admitting that he had touched me, "And so what?" I started sweating and shaking, I turned around again and stayed in line, quietly walking towards my sister and almost pushing her with my body. I could not say anything. I was paralyzed with fear and just wanted the line to move faster.

We took some steps forward and he got closer to me and did it again. I could not speak. I saw my sister leave the line and return to the table with my mother. I moved quickly and stood in front of my father, pretending that I wanted to grab some food from where he was. I could have left the line and followed my sister and my mother, but I did not. I was not thinking clearly until I made sense of it later. I was not aware of the food, only wondering about the people around us. I was very embarrassed and felt guilty. What if somebody saw what happened? It never occurred to me to tell my parents at that moment, "This person is touching me." On the contrary, I was embarrassed, as though *I* had done something wrong. Imagine the shame of saying what that man did to me. I knew that women experienced severe assaults and that this incident was meaningless compared to such cases. Even so, accusing him at the moment involved the verbalization of what he had done, and of the parts of my own body he had touched. My head was filled with guilty thoughts. Was it my changing body what sent those messages? I was hitting puberty, and I felt it was my fault—the way I was dressed. We had been warned about short skirts being inappropriate.

Had I invited him to touch me inappropriately? Maybe my choice of clothing gave him that signal. Perhaps I was standing too close to him. All of those thoughts came to my mind, thoughts in which I tried to find a way to justify the behavior of a man who was not only a stranger to me, but who also hurt me. I even considered the idea that I was invading his space. I did not say a word or touch my food during the whole meal. I was only thinking about how embarrassed I was. I was very angry at myself.

As I make meaning of that experience, I am able to identify how, for years, I genuinely thought I was responsible for such an incident. My understanding of masculinity and the role of women were highly influenced by the Catholic education that I received. Although I was not as close to church as some Catholics are, I really internalized how women had the obligation of displaying decency in their attire in order to protect themselves. I also believed women were responsible for protecting men from committing sinful acts. Within this toxic and patriarchal mindset, failing to do so implied that I somehow deserved what happened to me. Because it was a sinful action I thought it was partly my fault, and I stayed quiet.

I address silence within matters of sexuality as a critical element that has emerged in different ways throughout my life. This silence has also influenced my understanding of my gender and identity. Furthermore, in the experiences I narrate, privilege plays a critical role in the understanding and overcoming of issues that include sexual abuse and non-consensual physical encounters. For instance, I have had the opportunity to reach out to resources and take care of my mental health. I've also been work through trauma, confident that I will not be marginalized or discriminated against because of my identities in therapy.

My experiences with power, abuse, and hyper masculinity have not been the most violent or traumatic. Yet, reflecting upon them has allowed me to identify some of the patterns and understandings I have been constructing around boundaries and sexuality. Most importantly, I have realized how my meaning making of those experiences has translated to passing judgement upon others. I've found these reflections to be enlightening as I seek to identify the ways in which I have judged myself and justified the attackers, not only in this situation but in different cases. For years, I made excuses for strangers—men who have harassed me or touched my body without my consent, men who have felt entitled to my sexuality because they do not see boundaries when it comes to the female body. I had normalized the feeling of *deserving* what I had experienced: "Of course, I was wearing a short skirt! That would not have happened had I chosen a different piece of clothing." Such thought is not only toxic to me—as I assumed the responsibility for the abuse—but it also permeated my judgement toward other forms of gender violence. For instance, I would find myself passively normalizing the idea of women being blamed for the abuse they experienced.

Blaming the victim does not always look like the assumption *she was wearing a skirt, she was basically calling for it*. There are many other things we do and say that are equally harmful. For example, we question what women were doing by themselves in the middle of the night. Or, we wonder about their relationship with their abusers, as if that information would rationalize the situation as not abusive. And we normalize violence before challenging machismo within our immediate social circles. This mindset has fostered a culture of re-victimization in places like Ciudad Juarez, where victims are not only subject to the trauma of abuse, but also to societal scrutiny and judgement. As a community we have learned to defend the abusers by putting all of the responsibility on the victims. In Mexico, particularly in cities like Juarez, machismo remains unchallenged and stronger than ever. In most environments—educational, familial and religious (in my experience, Catholic)—toxic masculinity has been constantly protected by justifying the predatory nature of men. This is reinforced by the idea that women must carefully nurture and care for men around her, being mindful of herself and responsible for any negative outcome that results from consensual and non-consensual sexual experiences.

7 La Culpa

There is a part in Catholic mass in which we are supposed to acknowledge our sins and symbolically hit our chest with our fist. This is a symbol of acceptance—acceptance of the times in which we have wronged God by our sinful actions. We say *"por mi culpa, por mi culpa, por mi gran culpa,"* and we symbolically punish ourselves. In this part of the mass, people are encouraged to acknowledge our bad actions, reflect on them, and feel repentance. The space for reflecting on guilt is short. During this moment, also known as the act of contrition, we are given about a minute in which we are paying attention and actively participating in the ceremony. After this time period, we are supposed to feel lighter. Its purpose, as I remember, was to lessen the burden of a sinful life as we feel sorry about the bad things we have done.

La culpa in Spanish means *guilt*. Thus, it also means *fault* in the context of making a mistake that bears negative consequences. From a very young age in the Catholic community, we are told that we bear *culpa* from the moment we are born; we are all guilty. According to Catholicism, Jesus Christ died for the humanity. Because of this, we must get baptized as a ritual of protection and redemption for what they call "original sin." Such sin implies that all human beings are born sinners. This ritual goes back to the Adam and Eve passage in the Biblical Old Testament. Adam and Eve dared to eat the forbidden fruit. Spoiler alert: the fruit is a metaphor for sex. In the Old Testament, humanity did not fall to bits over a red apple.

The story of Adam's and Eve's journey from a naked paradise to a nudity-shaming earth was one of the first biblical passages I learned as a child. This biblical passage, as many others, enforces heteronormativity, white supremacy, and patriarchy (Joshi, 2006). Our catechism teachers narrated how Adam was created first; he looked exactly like God. Most of my old catechism books depicted Adam as a white, able-bodied man and Eve a blonde, able-bodied woman. According to this story, Adam was having a blast in paradise, he was hanging out with the animals, enjoying God's gifts, and being grateful for his existence. Yet, he needed a partner. God, took Adam's rib, and from his rib created Eve, a partner for him. A treat because he was being good. She was a complementary human being of the same species, but had different physical attributes. They enjoyed each other's company and the gifts that God had granted them. They were running around paradise without any sense of modesty, as their bodies were not yet tainted with sin. By the way, the illustrators of my catechism book did a great job addressing nudity in a children's book by placing bushes, fruits, rocks, animals, and other nature-like props to cover Adam and Eve's genitalia. This couple, that God had created in his own image, had everything they needed in life to be happy.

Adam and Eve had only one restriction. They were commanded: "Do not eat from the forbidden tree, the one in the middle of paradise." They could have everything they wanted, except for the fruit on that tree. One day, Eve was tempted by her curiosity to approach the tree and see what all the fuss was about. She contemplated its fruits and felt tempted to try them. She resisted for a while and was about to walk away, when she heard a voice. It was a snake talking to her and telling her how great that fruit was. The snake—the representation of temptation—convinced dumb Eve to eat the fruit with Adam, who innocently followed along. They both disobeyed God, who was not happy with their choice. Consequently, Adam and Eve started experiencing shame and the need to cover their bodies and hide. They knew that what they had done was a terrible act. God found them and kicked them out from paradise. Some teachers would be more descriptive than others, saying that there were thunders in the sky as God expelled these two from paradise and threw them onto planet Earth. On this planet, they would have to work to earn everything they needed. They would suffer and experience cold and heat. The closing warning of the story is powerful: "It will be painful to bring children to the world." Our catechism teachers not only used this story as a rationale as to why the entire humanity is tainted with sin, they also used it to explain why labor is painful for women—as a deserved punishment for provoking God's anger.

Because of Eve's mistake, which negatively affected poor Adam, humanity was charged with pain, diseases, and years and years of horrible destruction. Now humanity needed redemption (Velasco, 2016a). Baptism in the Catholic religion brings the release of original sin which, allegedly, we all hold from the moment we are born. These lessons, as I remember them, were accompanied by a variety of visuals that included Jesus Christ coming came to earth to spread peace, empathy, and forgiveness and also dying for humanity. This was necessary to mend the mistakes and sins that were being committed by those living godless lives.

During Lent, our teachers discussed the different actions, sacrifices, and traditions proper for honoring the Calvary—the place where Jesus was crucified—and the sacrifice Jesus made through the crucifixion itself. Lent is a period of 40 days that anticipates Jesus' resurrection. Within this time frame, the Catholic Church encourages its flock to let go of material possessions and toxic behaviors, all in honor to Jesus' sacrifice for humanity. During Lent, there are days in which we cannot eat red meat and there are traditional dishes that are proper of this season. There are several Lent resolutions that people engage in, for instance, some individuals stop eating sugar, and others go further and claim not to gossip (at least for 40 days). Many of the school lessons pertaining to Lent included acts and symbols that portray imagery of Jesus Christ nailed to the cross. There was a yearly enactment, *via Crucis* (called the *Way of the Cross* in English), in which actors recreated the painful journey of Jesus before and during his crucifixion. Throughout the reflections in catechism class, masses, and ceremonies, we were reminded of how all of this pain is our fault, our *culpa*.

La culpa is a pedagogical tool often used within the Catholic community in Mexico. We learn *la culpa* to show regret for presumed inappropriate and/or negative choices, feelings, and behaviors. However, the scope of socially acceptable and unacceptable behaviors rooted in *la culpa* has many layers and nuances. *La culpa* has a function beyond being a way for Catholics to suffer consequences and show remorse for violating the *do no harm* principle. It touches upon issues of sexuality, responsibility towards the church, familial roles and responsibilities, keeping in line with imposed gendered roles, and other expectations that good church members should follow. The umbrella of *inappropriate* things to do or say is very wide and it is rooted in patriarchal and heteronormative ideology that oftentimes marginalizes women, LGBTQI+ individuals, and individuals from non-Catholic religious backgrounds.

In this context, when *la culpa* does not work—and individuals do not show repentance or an intention to change who they are, how they feel, and their behavior—the Catholic community ends up disowning them. This happens at the micro and macro levels. For instance, someone who is perceived and judged as an outlier—for example, someone who refused to go to church can be disowned by their own family, because their family adheres to and practice the conservative and rigid values of Catholicism (Martínez, 2015). Such values are also reflected socially at a macro level. In Mexico, non-Catholic, non-heterosexual, non-binary, and non-conservative individuals are oftentimes attacked, erased, and marginalized in the name of Catholicism.

8   Religious Schooling and Sexuality

As a little girl, I learned quickly that I needed to cover myself and dress properly with two purposes: first for my own *safety* and secondly to demonstrate *decency*. Such principles permeated the curriculum. The lessons regarding sexuality that I learned throughout my schooling often fostered patriarchal behaviors such as victim-blaming. Girls, for instance, needed to display modesty by wearing a skirt the length of four fingers below the knee. We would also be reminded to close our legs while we were sitting down and to be mindful of the importance of our virginity and purity. We needed to stay *pure* until we found a man that loved us so that we could share our sexuality with him and only him.

In the 1990s, sexual education became mandatory for all schools affiliated with the Public Education Board in Mexico. This included private schools, as they must be accredited by the Public Education Board (SEP). Starting with 5th grade, our textbooks contained depictions of the human anatomy instead of plants, which were included in previous textbooks. These new books explained reproduction and sexuality in a more specific and graphic manner, which frightened a lot of our conservative parents, teachers, and religious leaders. The scandal was that fifth graders were being *exposed* to the imagery of the human body, and that was troublesome for our parents and teachers, as they belonged to generations which learned about sexuality empirically and behind closed doors. Some of them learned through the passing along of questionable information among peers. However, in school their sexuality lessons consisted of images of plants and bees and the process of pollination.

In both public and private sectors of Mexican education, teachers often have biases towards sex education, more so during the 90s, when teachers were not used to addressing sexuality as directly. Additionally, I assume that teachers in my school had to struggle with a very conservative curriculum, their own biases and internalized views regarding sexuality, and the new demands of the Public Education Board that specified what content to address. The expectations were that the teachers who had narrow conceptualizations and understandings of sexuality would suddenly become experts in delivering informative content. Furthermore, religious schools limited teachers' practices and rhetoric when addressing these issues. I doubt that my teachers in elementary and middle school had professional development in which they explored their own biases and ideologies around sexuality in order to challenge them, especially because the setting was Catholic.

We addressed anatomy and the potential risks of becoming sexually active, including diseases that we could get, "especially if we were not married." According to our elementary and middle school professors, abstinence and marriage were the only protection against diseases and unwanted pregnancies. Our sex education classes were often tainted with fear towards pregnancy, the pain of labor, viruses, and diseases, which were graphically illustrated. This last component usually included shaming discourse, in which teachers validated the idea that "girls who sleep around deserve to get infected" or "that's what they get for engaging in intercourse outside of the sanctity of marriage." Most negative outcomes and consequences of sexual activity targeted women as the potential victims. Yes, we did address some of the illnesses for men as well. We saw imagery of diseases that detailed what could potentially happen to men if they were to catch certain diseases. However, what I remember most was the discourse of purity and virginity around these topics, as if preventing diseases depended solely in women's attitudes and behaviors.

The discourse in sex education class was tainted with machismo and was violent towards women. These classes did not challenge the roles and most toxic beliefs around sexuality. Furthermore, the lessons were gender-binary and homophobic. Our teachers rejected the idea of gender and sexual diversity, so we did not really address those possibilities in class. And, because the school agenda was completely Catholic, we constantly heard how "God created a man and a woman so that they could be together." When I think about how I normalized this narrative, hearing it over and over, I consider all of the children whose identities were non-heterosexual and/or non-binary in terms of gender. These words meant very little to me at the time. I was not hurt by them as my identities were not questioned. As a child, I naturally internalized such rigidness regarding sexuality and relationships, and many of my peers did as well. Now I wonder how many of us have challenged such lessons in order to create safe spaces for every gender and sexual identity to exist. Not doing so has costed lives, as we continue to marginalize individuals through a hate speech that is disguised as *Godly* and *family-centered*.

Although the Public Education Board in Mexico recently communicated their intention to educate elementary and middle school students on issues of sexual and gender diversity, discrimination towards LGBTQIA individuals remains commonplace in our country (Pacheco, 2016). In Mexico, at least 76 members of the LGBTQIA community are murdered every year, solely for existing as gender non-binary and/or for not identifying as heterosexual individuals in the country (Bastilda & Navarro, 2018). Thus, including topics around gender and sexual diversity in textbooks will not suffice as long as the educational system does not challenge the biases of teachers and administrators, who at the end of the day, are in charge of enacting these pedagogies in their classrooms.

Since Catholicism is the most practiced religion in Mexico and this religion discriminates toward gender and sexual minorities, paying attention to the ways in which we exercise our power over others is critical. Nowadays in Mexico, non-heterosexual, non-binary and/or transgender identities continue to be treated as a joke or as wrong (Gutiérrez, García, Winton, & Margaret, 2018). The Catholic community has excluded these individuals not only from religious spaces but from their own families. Religion has the power of educating the masses; in the name of God, and millions of individuals have been disowned by their families and abandoned by their closed-minded community members. As a powerful majority and because of all of the harm that we have perpetrated, it is our responsibility as Catholics to identify and challenge the problematic areas of our own education. Further, we must acknowledge how it affects others who have been marginalized by our problematic practices and teachings.

CHAPTER 3

Imposed Gendered Roles

> Gender refers to a wide range of social/cultural meanings that are ascribed to sex categories. We like to think of gender as composed of both gender *identity* and gender *expression*. *Gender identity* refers to a person's internal self-concept with regard to gender categories like man, woman, transgender, genderqueer, and many others. Gender expression refers to behaviors, such as attire, demeanor, and language, through which we intentionally or unintentionally communicate as gender.
>
> CATALANO AND SHLASKO (2013, p. 426)

∴

A gender reveal announcement is a thrilling experience for many families in Mexico, particularly these days. We are so influenced by the trends in the United States, where people pop balloons and tiny pieces of pink or blue confetti announce the sex of the baby. In doing so, we get to immediately assign an unborn baby a personality based on binary gendered ideologies of the child being male or female (Applequist, 2014; Muskus, 2018). We rush to envision the personality of a boy or a girl based on their sex (Catalano & Shlasko, 2013), and the roles we envision go beyond the designation of pink and blue as genderappropriate colors. Based on this predominant gender binary ideology, children learn to normalize what society expects from them: what is considered normal and what is not. This is, according to Harro (2013), the first socialization, in which "We are socialized by people we love and trust, and taught to play to play our roles and follow rules" (p. 46). Girls, for example, will be encouraged to be fond of princesses. They are expected to display fragility and femininity, whereas boys will be physically strong, masculine, and brave. This includes the understanding that boys will not display emotions of vulnerability. Gender is an expectation of the expression of roles and behavioral characteristics. The culture in Mexico has strongly associated gender with sexuality, meaning that the rubric of behavioral expectations we must follow depends on the genitalia we are born with. Furthermore, such conceptualizations of gender seldom allow individuals to challenge the gender norms (Lozano-Verduzco, 2017). Boys being *too sensitive*, for example, is off the table.

When my mother was pregnant, the doctors told her I was going to be a boy. My family had already assigned me a name and had begun to envision my personality. My father quickly assumed that I would be into soccer, American football, and other *manly* things that we could share. The day I was born the doctors said: "We've made a mistake; she's a girl." My mother was thrilled. Though my father was happy, he admits that his concerns regarding parenthood changed dramatically. Suddenly, my father started worrying more, and his ideas with regard to our potential bond changed immediately. Perhaps his understanding of society in Mexico not being as kind to women as it is to men influenced his concerns. Though he grew up with two sisters, he constantly says that he had no idea how to interact and communicate with girls, much less how to raise them. My mother immediately adopted the role of caretaker. My mother often talks about an unspoken agreement that she and my father had, in which she would take care of my education, discipline, development, wellbeing, nutrition, and emotional issues. My father would be responsible for providing for our family.

"Boys are easier to raise" is a common statement made in Mexico, at least in my family. My parents have always been concerned about our safety as women. Throughout his life, my father, as most men in Mexico, has learned, adopted, reinforced, and benefited from patriarchal values and ideologies that strongly relate to how he treats, and what he expects from women. Therefore, there were many layers to his concerns—most of them rooted in patriarchal ideas of presumed female inferiority, helplessness and incompetence. He normalized these ideas because of his education, family values, and the ruling, prevailing culture of patriarchy. His mother stayed home and gave up her career to devote herself to her family, and his father was the economic provider of the household. My father's model of masculinity was one of endurance and of being the provider, but masculinity was also taught to him within a machista framework. The gendered roles in my father's household were fixed; women were expected to be homemakers and men earned the money. My father learned that men and women had different and specific roles, and that there are certain spaces that women *cannot* occupy.

My father's understanding was that, because I was a girl, I was going to have more challenges in life: difficulties finding a job, challenges succeeding in school, and having to navigate through a world that belongs to and is run by men. Though my father wanted my sister and me to have college degrees and learn English, he constantly joked about how he would have peace in his heart once my sister and I married a guy. His education shaped his ideologies regarding gender hierarchy and learned that women occupy lower positions, with some extraordinary exceptions. He has also normalized the fact that men are at the top of the social pyramid. Therefore, my financial security would entail depending on someone who could succeed at the top. His perception and understanding of gender roles is very traditional and it is deeply embedded in him. As with many people in Mexico, my father has been conditioned to think that women are helpless and need to be protected. It is always better if women are married to someone who is economically stable. My father likes the fact that I am pursuing a doctoral degree. He has stated that he is proud of me, nonetheless, our conversations regarding my education and future often end up with him making a joke about me marrying one of my engineer friends "with a future."

Instead of confronting my father's machismo, I used to feel disrespected and triggered by such insinuations and disappointed in his perceptions of my capabilities. My father trusting my engineer friends' competence and abilities over mine was devastating. As I learned about the gender hierarchical pyramid, I began to believe my father's narrative. I doubted my capabilities all the time. I used to question my career choices and worry about my future as an unmarried woman. Although marriage was never a dream of mine, I had internalized the idea that life is harder when you do not have a husband, as there is no safety net that can impede the inevitable fall. My family, school, society, and *my entire environment* validated such principles.

I would like to make clear that it is not my intention to villainize my father, who I deeply love and respect. Yet, I cannot address machismo and gender roles without describing the source of my first lessons regarding gender—which started at home. His intentions were never to consciously put me and my sister down, or make us think less of ourselves. In his mind, the best for us is to be with men who can support us the same way his father supported his mother, and the same way he has supported my mother. A culture of machismo and benevolent sexism has taught my father that intelligence, progress, freedom, and economic prosperity are masculine qualities. Now that I have grown up, I have had the opportunity of discussing issues of machismo with him. Although it has not been an easy task, I have had the opportunity of articulating my anger into a conversation in which he can see some of the toxicity in his rhetoric. Nonetheless, patriarchy is deeply ingrained within his mindset as it is in most men's in this country.

1 *La Familia es Primero*

Familial contexts exemplify machismo and the shape of gendered roles in Mexico (de la Rubia & Basurto, 2016; Medrano, Miranda, & Figueras, 2017). The lessons taught about what a woman ought to do are highly influenced by family heritage and values. *Familism* is the "strong bond of nuclear and extended family members, marked by feelings of loyalty, reciprocity and solidarity and desire to meet family expectations" (Espinosa-Hernández, 2015, p. 896). Though this is a cultural valued, coined by some researchers as a term of community, Espinosa-Hernández (2015) also refers to *familism* as one of the elements that contribute to female oppression, as it fosters the development of traditional gender roles.

My grandparents from both sides of the family grew up highly Catholic and conservative. Thus, their lives were highly influenced by religious principles that narrowed the opportunities for women. My mom's mother gave birth to nine babies and had one miscarriage. Because of several conversations with members of the Catholic clergy, grandma continuously blames herself for *haber abortado* [having an abortion]. Her lack of financial resources and education and her strong conservative Catholic background narrowed her life choices to marriage and motherhood. These circumstances shaped her life the same way they continue to shape the lives of many Mexican women who live in poverty. Lechuga, Guerrero, and Ramírez (2015) have stated that, historically, Mexican women have been expected to be mothers and homemakers. Any deviation of such expectation opens a door for questioning women's decency and their morality.

Such values were conveyed to my mother and her siblings, and all of them followed the pathway of marriage and family. Though my mother and most of her siblings were granted a college education, they built their lives around a heteronormative and *machista* culture, where most women remain in their households taking care of the children, and men were out working and providing for the family. My mom devoted herself to her family as soon as she married my father. My mother's wedding not only signified her commitment to my father and a celebration of their love, their wedding also included her agreement to cook, wash, iron, sweep, and mop after my father and her children.

Historically, maternity has been imposed as an inherent practice and purpose of life to women in Latin America (Palomar, 2005). Thus, if we don't have children by a certain age, or at all, we are perceived as incomplete—a waste of space, a uterus gone to waste—not woman enough. My mother did not get to enjoy her young adult life. Taking care of me and my sister, the commutes to school, and full responsibility for housekeeping chores took over her life. At some point both of my parents were working. Whether my mother was working or not, she was always responsible for the household and our education; disciplining us, looking for ways to teach us life lessons, making decisions as to where should we go to school, correcting our bad behavior, showing concern about our grades, establishing a relationship with our teachers, and much more. Those things, I learned, were women's responsibilities. If there was time to work, even better, but my mother never had the choice to pursue her career.

As we grew up, we learned the tasks of a woman in the household by observing what my mom did. I remember her frustration toward my dad or us when we were sloppy. She adopted her role as the one in charge of the house and everything being clean and ready. My sister and I had housekeeping responsibilities, yet we were always told that we were *helping* mom, as if it was not everyone's responsibility to keep a clean house, as if that role was hers exclusively. The conversation with regard to delegating housekeeping chores and activities would often turn into "One day, you will have to do this for your own family as well." I remember thinking about my future as someone's wife. I imagined the endless tasks I would have to perform, keeping the house clean and preparing meals. It was a nightmare, I never thought of marriage in a romantic way. I feared the day I had to do the same, to devote myself to a husband and children, forgetting about my own identity. I did not want to live my mother's experience. She was always scolding someone, stressing over our problems, and leaving her own for later. It seemed as if her life was ours completely. This was the main role model I had for how a woman, a wife, and a mother should be.

2   Marianismo and Machismo

Please beware that this section includes references that illustrate transphobic media content. *"El hombre llega hasta donde la mujer se lo permite"* [A man will go as far as a woman allows him]. I have been hearing and repeating this almost my entire life. Throughout my education, I internalized the idea that women must know when to stop and how to say no to men. On the other hand, men are rarely told not to rape or abuse women; it is often assumed that they will not do it. *Marianismo* is defined by Moral and Ramos (2016) as the attitudes of submission that women must assume in order to fulfill their role in society. In this context, female submission includes women perceiving themselves as highly spiritual and morally superior to men. These beliefs assign women responsibility for any sexual encounter and its consequences including pregnancy, illness, and violence (Englander, Yáñez, & Barney, 2012; Fuller, 2012).

Marianismo is a parallel term to machismo. *Marianismo* has its roots in Catholic and Christian religions, as women are expected to achieve a level of sanctity modelled by Virgin Mary. According to Shuck (2008), the Catholic church has traditionally encouraged women to follow the steps of Virgin Mary, and women have been suppressed. They are instructed not to follow their sexual instincts, which are denied. Elenes (2010) theorizes that the patriarchal *ideal* model of virginity that marianismo follows is rooted in the masculine perception, narrative, and idealization of Our Lady of Guadalupe. Such narrative portrays Our Lady of Guadalupe as a submissive, passive, and *good* woman who has lived in chastity and sanctity and should be a model for all Catholic women. Nonetheless, Chicana scholars such as Elenes (2010), have embarked on a quest of recuperating *mujeres* [women] such as La Virgen de Guadalupe, and reverting the meanings that patriarchal narrative has attributed to them. For example, under the male narrative that outlines the model of womanhood, women are expected to remain *pure* and save themselves for a single sexual partner and, of course, wait until marriage to engage in any type of sexual activity or behavior.

Marianismo dictates many responsibilities for women, as they/we are perceived as the ones in control of avoidance of sexual contact. This means that men can lose control and engage in sexual activity, but it is women's responsibility to stop them, as we have, per default, a "higher level of awareness" given by spirituality and faith. Therefore, if we do engage in sexual activities, experience rape or sexual molestation, it is our responsibility; we did not *say no* or *sent the wrong messages* by dressing or acting *improperly*.

"*A las mujeres no se les toca ni con el pétalo de una rosa.*" *Women should not even be touched with a rose petal.* We claim throughout this *dicho* (proverb) that we teach men about consent, by implying that men should respect women and not dare to touch us as we are *hyper delicate beings*. Yet, Mexico has extremely high rates of both physical and emotional violence towards women (Medrano, Miranda, & Figueras, 2017). Across contexts and environments, we continue to normalize gender violence. We keep dismissing women in vulnerable positions and LGBT+ people's experiences and risk of abuse by justifying toxic masculinity and by avoiding these issues. Through family traditions, machista discourse, and overall education, we have failed to hold men accountable for their actions; we have, in fact justified their actions by attributing acts of abuse and ignorance to men's gender. The "sanctity" of marriage has also prevented many women to get a marriage annulment, as in the traditional wedding vows, the couples promise unconditional love, which oftentimes becomes endurance of pain, physical and emotional violence.

Our cheesy and empty saying about *no tocar a una mujer ni con el pétalo de una rosa* [not touching women, not even with a rose petal] is seldom applied, especially when it comes to the transgender women community in Mexico. Before proceeding with this section, it is important to state the following: transgender women are women, and transgender men are men. As explained by Serano (2013), "*trans woman* is defined as any person who was assigned a male sex at birth, but who identifies as and/or lives as a woman" (p. 443). Including such as statement is critical as in Mexico, as in most parts of the world, transgender identities have been prosecuted, questioned, mocked and denied (Gutiérrez et al., 2018). Boivin (2014) reports that in Mexico "transgender individuals, more than any LGBT group, are victims of physical violence, work exploitation, and police brutality" (p. 105). Mexican society has blatantly dehumanized this part of the population, making survival almost impossible. Violence toward transgender individuals, particularly transgender women of color, has achieved a disturbing normalization (Catalano & Shlasko, 2013). There is a very popular song in Mexico as an exemplar—a song that keeps playing in graduation balls, quinceañeras, and weddings. People will listen to the cheerful rhythm and cumbia notes and stand up to dance with their partners immediately. The premise of the song is harassment, sexual assault, and violence against a transgender woman. This piece starts with a man singing how he saw a pretty girl and took her to the darkness to whisper and flirt with her. When she introduces herself to him, he notices that she has a deep voice and he wonders whether she is a man or a woman. Because this man had that concern and felt entitled, he—without consent of course—reached out and touched her. He then states how he realized he felt male genitalia. After inappropriately touching a person, he sings about running away and the difficulties having to deal with his friends' comments and mockery for approaching and flirting with a transgender woman. Finally, the singer states how his girlfriend knew about the incident, and that is why she broke up with him [the singer].

We dance to this song. We do not stop to question the content of the message prior to consuming and internalizing it. We sing along. We don't stop to question how is this problematic, or who are we hurting at the parties or spaces in which, neglectfully, these songs are being played. This song is about nonconsensual touching. It is immensely transphobic. It celebrates a toxic masculinity that we constantly overlook and feel comfortable ignoring, as the lyrics do not offend us personally. This song is only an example of how machismo, transphobia, and homophobia are deeply rooted in pop culture. Moreover, it is another form of normalizing violence toward a very marginalized group of people in our country and all over the world (Serano, 2013).

Women are taught that we have the power and obligation of stopping every sexual encounter, even if it is a forceful one (Medrano, Miranda, & Figueras, 2017). We quickly learn to take on the responsibility for abuse and, consequently, we pass judgement to other women who experience abuse. We question their morals and self-control, attributing violence to their inability to say no. From my experience with the Catholic church and community, this happens more often than it should. We feel like we have the moral authority to pass judgement on others. Women are not allowed to be sexual if we are not married and planning to have children. As Monsivais stated in 1995, "Chastity is the church ideal, sex practices are to remain exclusive of reproductive obligations" (p. 179). Though Monsivais' citation is more than 20 years old, it still applies to current times. Alas, the narrative has not changed much. *Marianismo* allows machismo to live on.

Policymaking and government are not the exception when it comes to enforcing machista behaviors in Mexico. Evelio Plata, former Mayor of Navolato Sinaloa in Mexico, held women accountable for high rates of teen pregnancy. In 2011 Mayor Plata proposed a ban on wearing miniskirts to prevent unwanted pregnancies among teenagers. He stated that teenagers dressing provocatively and the image that young women were displaying were basically invitations to have unprotected sex (El Economista, 2011). An example of marianismo and machismo colliding is when we as women, side with toxic masculinity and replicate the Mayor's rhetoric by comments such as: *"Muchacha tonta, debió tener más cuidado. En vez de ponerse a estudiar va y se embaraza"* [Stupid girl, she should have been more careful. Instead of studying she goes out and gets pregnant]. Doing so, we treat her as if she had gotten pregnant on her own, we question her intelligence, her self-control and her decency, and therefore all the burden and responsibility is placed on her. In this rhetoric, she, the woman, teenager and/or single mother, is always the "unintelligent one," the one who failed to endure and follow through her role of spiritual and moral superiority. As a society, we have learned that women are in control of what happens to them sexually, excusing toxic masculinity.

Alongside with machismo, *marianismo* denies sexuality as a pleasurable experience for women. Rather than enjoyment, the purpose of sexual activity should be solely for the purpose of conceiving. *Marianismo* requires women to be in control of themselves and their environments by fully ignoring their sexual impulses and desires. Furthermore, women must devote themselves to spiritual lives and wait to have sexual experiences until they are married. Then they can engage in sexual acts for the sole purpose of having children. Additionally, there is a premise grounded in the Catholic religion. Velasco (2016a) describes it as the iconic image of the Catholic Virgin Mary. And, in Mexico, La Virgen de Guadalupe has been used as an attempt to shape the behavior and actions taken by women. Specifically, the expectations are for them to become homemakers and mothers, having measured freedoms—such as having a job or becoming educated—as long as they fulfill their gendered responsibilities.

Reluctance to adhere to one's assigned responsibilities on the basis of gender implies negative consequences. "As a consequence of machismo and *marianismo*, men have the right to punish their partner when she deviates from her expected roles of submissiveness and servitude" (Moral & Ramos, 2016, p. 40). Though a Catholic priest will never encourage husbands to beat or abuse their wives, their narrative will be permissive to men and enforce the place of each gender in a hierarchical order. For instance, going to a Mexican Catholic middle-class wedding is usually a clear example of machismo and patriarchal narratives being enacted. My experiences attending Catholic weddings of friends and family members have allowed me to reflect upon several issues that occur during the ceremony: (a) Catholic priests have encouraged women to be patient with their husbands, to take care of their money for the sake of the family, and to obey them and respect them as the lord commands; (b) men are praised for their choice of raising a family and sharing their heart with a woman; and (c) couples have been encouraged to have as many children as God wants, which means contraception is not allowed. This is the *right* way to do things. Catholic middle-class White Mexican women have many more privileges and opportunities than do Women of Color. Narrating the discourses that are enacted during weddings does not have the purpose of portraying them/us as victims, but to exemplify how we as women judge and criticize other women's decency and choices. Furthermore, it is important to clarify that my experiences with the Catholic church do not define all marriage ceremonies or Catholicism in general. Nonetheless, I see it as important to critique and identify the narrative and messages behind the traditions that surround us as women, particularly Mexicanas.

Dominant patriarchal messages are not only embedded within religion, but also media, cultural traditions, and a history of normalizing patriarchy. As Moctezuma, Narro, and Orozco stated in 2013, approximately 57% of women aged 15 years old and older are married or live with a male partner and are very likely to experience domestic violence. According to *Encuesta Nacional sobre la Discriminación en México*, also known as ENADIS [National survey regarding discrimination in México] (ENADIS, 2010), 24% of the female population in Mexico who share a household with a male partner feel obligated to ask for authorization to spend money. Additionally, 44% reported to have a need to ask for their partner's permission to leave the house unaccompanied, and 10% of the women interviewed reported a need to request their partner's consent to use any type of contraceptive. A study conducted by the Mexican Census Bureau (INEGI) in 2011 indicated that approximately 44.9% of women in Mexico who live with their male partners and/or are in a relationship reported to have experienced some type of violence including physical, economic, emotional, sexual, and psychological violence. Such statistics demonstrate a normalcy experienced by almost half of our population on a continuous basis.

As a consequence of machismo, Chihuahua is the state with the highest rate of violence against women. In Chihuahua, 80% of the female population state have reported experiences of abuse (Aboites, 2012).

Machismo is evident in many forms and manifestations. For reasons of practicality, I am outlining three categories of its manifestation: (a) *micro-machismos* can be considered a mild starting point of unnoticeable violence, oftentimes disguised as chivalry (Moral & Ramos, 2016); (b) verbal abuse, psychological violence, and physical harassment; and (c) feminicide—the violent act of murdering women—which is the worst in terms of the outcome for women and society (Berlanga, 2015).

Micro-machismos are benevolent forms of sexism, they have an unconscious intention of limiting the women's ability of choosing. Micro-machismos can be demonstrated by a wide variety of behaviors and attitudes. Some examples of this include presuming and verbalizing that women are incompetent to succeed in some careers, driving vehicles, and using technology. Another manifestation of this kind of sexism is attributing failure to gender. Rodriguez, Rodriguez, and Ramírez (2004) state that this type of machismo is not always evident, as it often poses as chivalry. Machismo and presumed *caballerismo* [chivalry] often merge. Machismo denies the relevance of women. A *caballero* may display behaviors of respect towards women, including attention toward women and a focus on familial values that often define the *woman's place*. A protective male is in charge to allow or deny a woman her access to the social world, using phrases such as "you are the queen of the house" denoting the cues and reinforcement of dominance and highlighting the freedom and limitation of women.

Harassment and physical violence have the main goal of perpetuating and maintaining hierarchical relationships on the basis of gender. According to a study conducted by the Mexican Census Bureau (INEGI, 2011), every year more than five million women experience aggressions such as catcalling and sexual slurs. Additionally, over one million women reported being groped and touched without their consent by strangers in different locations and contexts.

Catcalling is one of the most common and visible forms of violence towards women in Mexico. Most of the time catcalling is experienced by women who walk to work or take public transportation. As women, we expect catcalling if our commutes involve walking or taking public transportation. Privilege is an important component of this part of this issue as well. It is interesting how, as Mexican women, we normalize all types of violence and abuse towards the *others*—the ones who are not like us, not the middle and upper classes. Alas, we have not achieved a level of self-critique and reflection in which we can understand phenomena if it does not directly affect us.

In the middle of my undergraduate program, I spent a semester in Guanajuato as part of a mobility program among Mexican universities. I was walking and taking the bus everywhere. I experienced my share of catcalling, which is minimal compared with other women who have always had the need to walk and use public transportation to commute. I was walking everywhere by choice, because I chose to move away from my city and experience college somewhere else, but I always had the possibility of going back home where I had resources and safety. Most women in Mexico who are victims of this form of violence do not have this privilege and these choices. During spring break, my parents came to visit; we agreed to meet in a little plaza downtown. I was walking towards the plaza with my friends, and suddenly a group of middle-aged men, who were leaving one of the cafes in the plaza, started yelling things about our bodies and what they would do to us "if they could."

We were scared and angry, as it did not matter where we moved to. They followed us and continued verbalizing how much they wanted to have our bodies. And even though the plaza was filled with people, they kept yelling their sexual desire towards us. Suddenly I saw my parents coming towards us. A golden opportunity, I thought, they will see that we are not alone. I walked towards my dad, and suddenly these men were petrified. I told my father "Those guys are harassing us; they are yelling sexual slurs at us." My dad remained speechless and looked at those men. They were pale and scared, as they thought my father was going to come at them and confront them. To their surprise, he did not.

We kept walking towards the exit of the plaza as if nothing happened. I was glad to see them sweat and shutting up, as they saw me pointing out their behavior. Yet, I was very disappointed with my father not speaking up. Now that I reflect upon that experience, I do not think I was surprised at his reaction. We even had a huge fight about how violence was never the answer to these issues. "What do you want me to do? Hit them? I am not going to pick a fight." he said. He was angrier at me for confronting him than at those men for harassing me. He insinuated that making a scene and using violence was not the solution. He argued that we cannot educate everyone in the world and that I must ignore people's words and move on. I was certainly not expecting that my father physically confront those men. But I did want him to confront them verbally. Obviously, my friends and I were powerless in the situation. It did not matter what we would have said to them, they would not have stopped yelling and following us. My mother did not say much either. She was more concerned about trying to calm me down so that I would not make a scene in public. She was also encouraging me to let go of the situation, as my father said: "we must let it go." The lack of action and response denied the validity of my anger and frustration. Furthermore, my father's passive attitude gave these men the power of getting away with harassment and verbal violence.

My father's disregard towards those men, and my mother's lack of intervention and passive anger, are only one example of how we have internalized hyper-masculinity and machismo, and how it shows as part of life. I do not tell this story to victimize myself or as a personal example of what gender violence looks like. I chose to share this experience to illustrate the permissiveness granted from one man to another when there is an aggression. My father was not related to the men who were harassing us. He did not even know them, and he preferred to have a conflict with me than to confront those men. I see machismo as a disease that most of us carry, particularly heterosexual Mexican men and women. We all embody patriarchy in different ways because that is what we have learned throughout our lives.

My father's reaction and my mother's passiveness are only examples, but there are other ways I have been impacted by machista ideologies. Indeed, I, myself, have taken up these ideologies at certain times. I was young and very immature. I thought for a minute that perhaps I had brought the situation on me: *maybe I should not dress in a certain way*. This is the way I would judge other women who would get pregnant as teenagers. I would not bother to go beyond the context or situation of an individual before passing judgement. *She should have been more careful, it is not like we don't know about contraception.* I would not hesitate to judge the lives of other women who had not had my privileges and resources. I would not stop and think about their status of vulnerability, mental health or how they had probably been victims of manipulation and deceptive discourse from older men. I have often enacted machismo and judged other women.

Not only men, but also women in Mexico, have perpetuated a narrative in which it is implied that victims of harassment and rape called for the aggression (Jeppesen, 2015). The implication is that this could have been avoided if they were dressed in a discreet way or were not walking by themselves at night. Men tend to be excused for acting on their *instincts*, and women always carry the burden of being the *rational ones*. Within this mindset, when sexual aggression happens, women are the ones who should have done things differently. Women need to learn how to be careful and prevent these things from happening.

In Ciudad Juarez, as in many other parts of the world, feminicides are the worst consequences of machismo behavior (Jeppesen, 2015). As a society, we've enabled the government to look away from these cases. We have become numb to them, particularly because when belonging to more than one privileged group, we rarely see feminicide as a potential personal risk. Feminicide is the misogynistic act of murdering women, and it has been occurring in Mexico for a long time. It is important to add that feminicides and the way they are addressed in Ciudad Juárez are highly correlated to race and class. In Ciudad

Juarez, most of the victims of feminicide are working-class or low income Women of Color (Navarrete, 2016). The occurrences of femicide among this population have been highly neglected by Mexican authorities (Incháustegui, 2014; Jeppesen, 2015).

In Mexico, machismo informs impunity and neglect. An example of such is Alejandro Garcia Ruiz, an ex-deputy from the Institutional Revolutionary Party in Chiapas, Mexico. In 2014, while discussing corruption in a radio show, Ruiz said: *"Todas las leyes tienen lagunas. Y como se dice, desgraciadamente, la ley es como las mujeres, se hicieron para violarlas"* [All laws have loopholes. And you know what they say, unfortunately, the law is like women; they are both meant to be violated] (Proceso, 2014, para. 3). The normalcy promoted by this rhetoric is problematic. Through his narrative, Garcia Ruiz denied the severity of sexual abuse towards women.

As Lugo pointed out in 1985, "The jurisdictional system has become a key element in women's oppression, as it controls her sexuality, marginalizes women and their family, and it impairs their chances of freedom and independence" (p. 46). Unfortunately, 30 years after this statement such conditions remain almost intact in our society, given the large number of unresolved cases in which women have been raped and murdered all over Mexico.

Villaseñor-Farías and Castañeda-Torres (2003) encountered several ways in which teenagers in Mexico blame victims of machismo and sexual violence. Such teenagers were surveyed, and according to this study, blamed women for being too pretty and/or flirty; walking alone in the streets at night; being prostitutes (addressing sex work in a derogatory and dismissive way); not knowing how to say no; and not being able to draw the line. This study is an exemplar of how we, as community members continue to justify violent practices—normalizing a machista mentality leads us to blame victims, particularly women, for being attacked, assaulted, or raped.

Class and race are harsh indicators of the risks posed by machismo, femicide, and gender violence (Garduño, 2016). Women with fewer resources, including Indigenous women in Mexico, experience higher rates of life threats, morbidity, and mortality on the basis of gender (Moctezuma, Narro, & Orozco, 2013).

In Ciudad Juarez, over 1600 cases of femicide have been documented since 1993 (El País, 2016). Mostly, underprivileged women are the ones who have been taken away from their families (Ruiz, 2015). For example, women from lower socioeconomic classes are made more vulnerable by riding the bus late at night, working in a factory, and walking by themselves. The families of the victims not only struggle with the loss of their daughters, but with societal views regarding their daughters from which all of us in Mexico are responsible for. There is still a large portion of the population that questions these cases and put the responsibility on the victims: *"Y luego por qué las violan"* [No wonder why they are raped]. Almost every *Juarense* has heard this phrase at least once when addressing feminicide, as if such type of violence could be avoided by the victim, as if these women had put themselves at risk solely by existing. *Juarenses* [individuals who are from Ciudad Juárez] with privilege, privileged Mexicans who live in the border and get to witness this type of violence through the news, are often entitled to voicing negative opinions and blaming women for being attacked, harassed and murdered.

hooks (2010) addresses sexism and the way women engage in it as we move forward and judge other women upon their choices, lifestyles, limitations, and experiences. Saying that low-income women deserved rape and murder, is a blatantly sexist act that continues to impede the development of a true sisterhood. As long as we continue to use terms such as *decency and morals* when discussing issues of gender violence and referring to the victims of feminicide, we are doing a disservice to them—re-victimizing them. There is a need to unlearn the concept of *decency* and *morals* as attributes that presumably belong to the highly religious/Catholic and higher socioeconomic classes. These conceptualizations have contributed to the neglect towards gender violence and the normalization of rape within marginalized populations in Ciudad Juárez. This, I believe, is one of the limitations of middle class, academic, and scholarly feminism in Mexico. As long as I claim to be a feminist solely because I want equal wages and to have the same opportunities as men, my feminism will continue to do nothing for the families of the victims of rape and femicide—populations who live in a constant state of vulnerability. While I may fight for the right to work, these women and their families have been working—probably since they were children due to necessity.

Though there are variations and cultural differences, one of the social norms for women in Mexico establishes that if you are a woman, you must leave your family when you get married. *Salir de blanco.* You must get married in white to signify your virginity. Many Mexican families use *la vergüenza* as a pedagogical tool, a resource that educates women by controlling and judging our behaviors—particularly sexual ones—through shame. *La vergüenza* can be understood as "the sexual guilt and lack of knowledge about sex" (Espinosa-Hernández, 2015, p. 604). *La vergüenza* is a shameful feeling that conditions women to behave in a certain way. Catholic women in Mexico are then conditioned to avoid being sexual with anyone unless they are married. In marriage, sex must only happen to create new life. Through *la vergüenza*, women learn to judge other women. We often embody machismo and feel entitled to measure other women based on patriarchal standards. Some of us excel at *slut shaming* as we scrutinize other women's habits, behaviors, attires, and relationships and claim ourselves to be morally superior. We too, have perpetrated machista ideologies in which we think we have a say about the experiences of women who experience rape, harassment, and/or domestic violence. We also judge single mothers, women who have been through divorces, and women who, according to our own patriarchal standards, *haven't done things right*. Presumed moral superiority has allowed us to condone machismo and to segregate and harm other women.

Within the machista narrative, particularly within the Catholic framework, heterosexual men in Mexico are conveniently not considered as spiritually elevated as women. Thus, la *vergüenza* is seldom used to educate them as it educates women. For instance, Mexican heterosexual men are often motivated to objectify and conquer as many women as possible. They will be rarely shamed or confronted for having too much sex or having too many partners. As women and under the machista rhetoric that we have adopted and perpetuated, the main argument is that there is only so much we can do and this is the way men are. Since patriarchy is also ingrained in our mindsets, we have been condoning these behaviors by failing to hold men accountable for their actions. Among men, the narrative shifts to the appraisal of hyper-sexual and hyper-masculine behaviors. La *vergüenza* operates differently in the sense that those men who are shamed, are the *mandilones*, which means a man that can be a pushover, someone who is handled by his woman partner. Such a term is also used to describe someone who care for a family, are monogamous, participate in housekeeping chores. This shame also applies to any men who dares to challenge perceived heteronormativity with their actions and behaviors.

"*Mi'jo ya tiene novia, ya le gustan las muchachas*" [My son already has a girlfriend, he is into girls now] said the proud father of one of my seven-year-old cousins. We all listened to this as though it were normal, and there were even a couple of laughs in the room. From a young age, boys are pressured to be attracted to girls, develop hyper-masculine attitudes, and hide their emotional vulnerability (Martínez, 2016). Fulfilling these criteria makes boys, society, and family members feel proud and safe. *They are just being boys*. This is problematic in several ways. First, our society continues to separate gender in a strictly binary manner and perceives homosexuality and non-binary gender identities as puzzling and shameful. Oftentimes, the support, love, and pride your family has for you as a Mexican person depends considerably on your alignment with heterosexual orientation. It also requires you to adhere to binary gendered roles. If there is a non-heterosexual, non-conforming, non-binary or transgender person in the family, it will not be unusual for family members in Mexico to ice that individual out because of the discomfort that comes along with their ignorance and prejudice.

I remember the appraisal that my cousins would get when they started dating. Even before then, my uncles would tease them with jokes about *getting* a lot of girls, having lots of female friends and not committing to any of them. They were just having fun. My cousins were still very young when they started being encouraged to enjoy their lives in this way. "*Disfruta pero ten cuidado*" [enjoy but be careful]. This was more than encouragement to experience their sexuality in a responsible way. "Enjoying carefully" also meant using and objectifying women carefully so that they wouldn't have to deal with unwanted pregnancies and sexually transmitted diseases. Additionally, these conversations always took place with the assumption that my cousins were heterosexual, labeling them as such from a very young age, *as they should be*. Yet, I do not recall anything being said about the importance of consent, respect towards women, or the possibility of having a same sex partner, being non-binary or non-conforming as part of these narratives. Furthermore, never has anyone in my family told me or my sister to hurry and have safe sex or to have some fun at men's expense just to figure out what we like and dislike sexually. This is because as noted by Gil-Romo and Coria (2007), gender inequalities in Mexico are manifested in different ways including the distribution of roles and cut-throat designation of responsibilities on the basis of gender and the inequitable opportunities for men and women to make choices about their own lives.

Currently in Mexico, there is not a lot of room for flexibility regarding the ideal model of masculinity. If boys show themselves as emotional, sensitive, and vulnerable, they will be immediately perceived as "not masculine enough" or "not men enough." From such *machista* assumptions, many derogatory terms that allude to homosexuality have been normalized. For instance, cisgender men (and women) keep using homophobic slurs to point out behaviors that do not fit their cookie cutter concept of masculinity. This practice reinforces the comfort and superiority that heterosexual people holds as a dominant group in Mexico.

3   A Feminism That Does Not Work for Everyone

Although women have been increasing our social participation throughout different power spheres in Mexico, we are far from achieving gender equity. We have been reluctant to explore the different layers and privileges that allow only cisgender women to occupy spaces of power, and marginalizes Women of Color, Indigenous women, women with disabilities, and transgender women in Mexico. My own experience, as a doctoral student in the United States, does not represent the realities of most women in Ciudad Juárez and in Mexico as a whole.

There is a need to acknowledge class, race, gender identity and sexual orientation, age, and physical abilities as elements that influence discrimination and gender violence. My early conceptualizations and ideas about gender were highly influenced by my education, including my Catholic education. Furthermore, my education also influenced a level of comfort and, therefore, a lack of action in working to achieve equity for all women. Again and again, patriarchy and heteronormativity have worked in my favor. They have done so in the same way they've worked for many other women who do not live in the margins of poverty or who are not facing the repercussions of racism. Nonetheless, the passivity of comfort does not only hurt society, it perpetuates the marginalization of women and individuals who have fewer privileges. It is critical to ask this question here; "how do I benefit from the different forms of oppression?" It is not a comfortable move to acknowledge how I have perpetrated gender violence through my passiveness. It is also difficult to recognize that for a long time I chose not to challenge my belief system—a belief system that situates me in a place of power and advantage over others.

LGBTQ+ issues, as well as race issues continue to be taboo topics in Mexican society, even among so-called feminists. We like to think that we have grown and moved forward into modern ways. We state to have gay friends and thus proclaim ourselves to be progressive and open-minded; but it is not the case, we still have a long way to go in order to enact a feminism that truly serves all populations.

In Mexico, the feminist movement has numerous adversaries, for instance the way in which patriarchy, religion, policy and other systems of oppression assert and replicate conservative values that are not compatible with equity. Religions such as Catholicism promote ideas such as women being obedient to their husbands; remaining at home and having as many children as God sends; caring for the family within a framework of *respect and love*; and living a godly life. Feminism also fights constantly against the most radical anti-feminist institutions and individuals—Mexican men, for instance, have given strength to the term *"femi-nazis."* This rhetoric blatantly compares feminism with Nazism, as if feminism sought to eradicate the lives and rights of men. Feminism is constantly mocked, targeted by individuals who devalue the work of women seeking equity. These critics portray feminists as violent, rude, and dangerous individuals whose cause is not worth fighting. As women, we have also impeded the development of a feminism that truly serves to marginalized groups in an equitable manner. We have replicated a feminism that solely serves the needs of the upper classes, neglecting our contribution to different systems of oppression in Mexico, such as racism and classism. As a Mexican woman, not only have I learned how patriarchy works, I have embodied it as well; passing on judgement towards other women, failing to scrutinize my privilege, and claiming to be a feminist solely when it has been convenient for me. As a white-passing Mexican, I do benefit from the patriarchal system.

Feminism in Mexico often does a disservice to marginalized communities, an example of this is how we fail to acknowledge the humanity of transgender women, or how we fail to challenge our internalized racism and let those values permeate through "our work." We are lacking accountability by focusing solely on those issues of gender that directly affect ourselves and people who share our spaces and environments. Since academic research and knowledge is highly valued in Mexico, the experiences of Black and Indigenous women have been constantly put aside in discussions around feminism. As scholars we have failed to acknowledge our own privileges, which include class, race, and even gender privilege, over vulnerable groups. Such gaps have permeated through our academic work and its limited scope.

Accountability with regard to issues of racism and discrimination is critical for White and white-passing Mexican women when it comes to understanding the oppression of Women of Color and Indigenous women and other marginalized communities in Mexico. Our research-informed feminism, which we post in our social media, has not served vulnerable groups of women. This is particularly true because we have not taken the time to unlearn and unpack our own experiences of privilege in order to achieve equality, much less equity. Mexican women have learned to identify whiteness as beauty, purity, innocence, and goodness. Consequently, we measure and judge other women by those standards. You might find many Mexican White women in positions of power, directing a corporation or owning a business, but having Indigenous women cleaning their homes. Does this feminism really help all women? How much do we still need to unpack? Why have we not done it? I believe it is simply because we do not see it as something convenient for us; because we do not want to give away our power; and because we do not want to admit that our narrative, opinions and discourse have been critical in the perpetration of gender violence towards Women of Color, undocumented women, transgender women, single mothers, Indigenous women, etcetera.

Whiteness is a critical component when talking about gender oppression. This is especially the case because the experiences of a White or white-passing Mexican are not the same ones as the experiences of a Brown or Black Mexican. Being reluctant to feel uncomfortable or not wanting to be the villain impedes us from seeing that, as White and white-passing Mexican women, we have failed to work towards equity. This is further intensified if we examine issues of class as well. Being a white-passing Mexican, has allowed me to smoothly navigate multiple systems without the obstacles that both Mexico and the United States have imposed towards People of Color. The machismo I have experienced cannot be compared to the pileup of discrimination, oppression and violence that Women of Color experience in Mexico on a daily basis, particularly when they are working class or low income.

Over the last decades, Women of Color in Mexico have had scarce opportunities to acquire equal levels of empowerment and representation in the power spheres. Media, politics, science technology, engineering, and mathematics (STEM), higher education, medicine, and health sciences—to name a few—are all fields of study and occupations dominated by men (Rodríguez, Domínguez, Pérez, Montano, & Salazar, 2016). Nonetheless, gender inequality issues cannot be narrowed down solely to those fields. Approximately 8.1% of women in Mexico are illiterate and a third of the female population in Mexico cannot count on any kind of health service (Moctezuma, Narro, & Orozco, 2013). Thus, Indigenous women and Women of Color who live within marginalized communities experience higher risks of abuse, rape, neglect, sexually transmitted diseases, and teen pregnancies (D'Emilio & Freedman, 2012).

Generally, as a whole, women in Mexico continue to be labeled as a vulnerable group solely because of their gender. However, there is invisibility around the circumstances of Women of Color and Indigenous women who are among the most vulnerable and disregarded populations (Moreno, 2017), and experience higher risks of being raped or assaulted. Both education and discourse have a great impact on the perceptions we have regarding female bodies. A nationalist and machista culture fed by media, history, and inequalities continues to imply that Women of Color are, or should be, voiceless, ignorant, incompetent, and defenseless.

Machismo is not solely enacted by men, for we have also internalized patterns of toxicity in which we have learned about "our place" and "the place" of *other* women. We, as women, create barriers towards other women who embody non-privileged identities (race, class, ethnicity, religion, and etcetera), question women's decision-making, scrutinize their mistakes, lives and choices, wonder about their children or lack-of, and about their partners and lack-of. Moreover, machismo and toxic masculinity, throughout the different systems, do not affect all women equally, which is why I believe we have been so negligent and uncritical in analyzing issues of feminism, power relationships and justice. For instance, for a racially and socioeconomically privileged woman in Mexico, machismo in a workspace is almost a given, yet such toxicity will not intersect with racial and or ethnic discrimination. Therefore, in a male-dominated system that is also racialized, the racially and socioeconomic privileged women still hold a significant amount of power over Women of Color who are working class or low-income.

In Mexico, many of us love to claim that we enact feminism and often like to say that we fight for our rights as a gender, claiming that we want equality, yet we have failed to get involved in issues that go beyond our convenience and identities. We keep letting our comfortable privileges, internalized racism, prejudices, learned shaming attitudes, to get in the way of us enacting a feminism that truly promotes justice and equity for all women.

CHAPTER 4

Racism in Mexico: *Ojos que no ven, corazón que no siente*

> Racism is the set of institutional, cultural, and interpersonal patters and practices that create advantages for people legally defined and socially constructed as "white," and the corollary disadvantages for people defined as belonging to racial groups that were not considered Whites by the dominant power structure in the United States.
>
> CASTAÑEDA AND ZÚÑIGA (2013, p. 58)

∴

Castañeda's and Zúñiga's explanation of racism is applicable to Mexico. According to Schmelkes (2006), Mexicans will never acknowledge their/our own racism, as there is a general lack of understanding of what racism means and a reluctance to identify it in all its forms. In Mexico, it is commonly thought that racism belongs exclusively to European and American cultures. Nevertheless, the marginalization and inequalities existing between Indigenous groups and People of Color indicate that racism is a problem that must be faced in order to achieve equity (Moreno Figueroa, 2016; Rico, 2016). In Mexico, the color of our skin is strongly tied to privilege and advantages (Navarrete, 2016). White and white-passing individuals are the ones who are positively represented on the Mexican media on the daily basis, our skin tone is not subject to mockery and subjugation throughout oppressive portrayals.

For a long time it was a very convenient argument for me to say that the biggest problem in Mexico was classism and not racism, as if both issues were separated from each other. Furthermore, as with many similarly privileged White and White-passing Mexicans, I failed to reflect upon racism being enacted in Mexico, because as many other White people I did not want to be called a racist. However, separating classism from racism, xenophobia, and ethnocentrism has allowed a color-blind culture in Mexico, in which we attribute all the problems and inequities to class disparities.

Many Mexicans that I know—Mexicans, in Mexico, who are White—often fail to understand that Mexican refers to a nationality, not a race. We struggle with the concept of whiteness. We often attribute the word white to ethnicity and nationality, assuming that only Caucasian individuals from Europe can be labeled as White, especially and conveniently during conversations that address issues of racism. Being Mexican and White are not mutually exclusive. Being Mexican and being a racist are definitely not mutually exclusive either. Such a statement might not need to be explained, but in Mexico, we desperately need to hear, read and understand these differentiations.

I am a White-passing Mexican, I have the option of choosing the tone of my skin depending on how long I stay under the sun. Because of this, I will always experience the existing privileges and comforts that come with my identities. The color of my skin tone does not challenge the white supremacist and racist standards that prevail in both Mexico and in the United States, where I currently live. Although there is discrimination that is language-based and biased towards people in Mexico, our whiteness can be a *wild card* under our sleeves; that is to say, we can easily pass as Caucasian. In both countries, we have smoother transitions and fewer challenges than People of Color throughout different systems and spaces (Castañeda & Zúñiga, 2013). I have been living in the United States for over five years, and I have never experienced racism. This is not because my university does not have that problem, but because I—as many other White Mexicans—am not a target of that particular form of oppression.

Ojos que no ven, corazón que no siente is a popular Mexican saying which means: if your eyes do not see it, your heart will not feel it, or *out of sight, out of mind*. I chose to highlight this saying, because it accurately represents how we, those with white or white-passing skin in Mexico feel and act regarding racism. For centuries, we have chosen not to see racism as a problem that we have, and therefore we do not see a need to improve or examine our behaviors. As stated by Schmelkes (2006), Mexicans will never acknowledge their own racism, as we commonly believe and claim that racism belongs exclusively to the United States and European countries.

Acknowledging that racism is a common form of oppression in Mexico has been a task oftentimes neglected by white and white-passing individuals in Mexico. We continue to perpetuate discrimination based on skin color. Black Mexicans were included in the Census for the first time in 2016 (Fundación Sur, 2016). According to the Mexican Census Bureau, about 1.5% of the population in Mexico identifies as Black and/or Afro-descendent (INEGI, 2017b). Yet, Mexico has historically operated around white-centered values, erasing the presence of Black Mexicans. According to Zárate (2017), Blackness in Mexico continues to be addressed as a foreigner identity to our nationalist depiction of what a Mexican looks like, further demonstrating how representations of

Black people are usually racist and stereotypical. It is not my place to even attempt to portray or describe the experiences of Black people in Mexico, yet, as someone who automatically benefits from unchallenged racism in Mexico, it is my responsibility to bring up issues of race when having conversations with my family, friends, and acquaintances.

In Mexico, people continue to label a baby as pretty or ugly based on the baby's race and whiteness. From the moment a child is born, family, friends and acquaintances comment on the baby's whiteness; the whiter the child is, the prettier they are considered. When I was born, close family members and friends told my mom they thought I would be whiter. My parents are both very white, and people were expecting me to be a whiter newborn. My mother received several comments like: "*que raro, pensé que iba a estar güerita*" [That's odd, I thought she would be whiter/blonde]. These statements were accompanied by a slight tone of disappointment. Someone even told my mother "not to worry," as my skin could become lighter as I grew up. This example does not illustrate me being a victim of racism or being discriminated against. It does illustrate how Mexican society continues to link whiteness with beauty—if my whiteness did not fulfill the expectations of my parents' acquaintances then, it is a good demonstration of their mindsets and biases regarding People of Color.

Are we, White Mexicans, aware of how whiteness bestows privilege across the world? Most of the time we are not aware. We seldom recognize our privileges, much less examine our own biases and the ways in which we have used it to our advantage. In these ways, we have contributed to the oppression of marginalized groups, including People of Color. Racism in Mexico is treated like a secret or a rumor that some people choose to believe and others do not because they do not endure it.

It is not that the evidence is not out there. In Mexico, whiteness is still considered a valuable resource throughout different systems. A recent study conducted by the Mexican Census Bureau (INEGI, 2017a), demonstrated a strong relationship between individuals having a white, light, or white-passing skin tone and their likelihood of occupying a position of power. Conversely, individuals of Color—Brown and Black Mexicans—tend to occupy lower positions and earn less income. This is a correlational study. Therefore, the Mexican Census Bureau, also known as Instituto Nacional de Estadística y Geografía (INEGI, 2017a) does not attribute race to success or lack of success. However, the study establishes that a connection exists between these elements. This finding generated a backlash among Mexicans. We were being accused of being racist! *How does the Mexican Census Bureau dare to make such accusations? That is a problem that the United States has, not us...do we?* Being White in Mexico, as in the rest of the world, comes with many benefits, and this study attempts to call Mexico out on its racism and racist history. These attempts have been rejected by the Mexican population. For White Mexicans, it is important to acknowledge our whiteness through an examination of the advantages and power that being white provides and affords us. We must also recognize how we have failed to challenge such power because we have found it beneficial. For instance, being White means that we fit the standards of socially defined beauty. Additionally, aspirational imagery represents whiteness in a positive way throughout the media and our intelligence or capabilities are not questioned on the basis of the color of our skin. Therefore, of course, we do not see racism as our problem. Doing so would entail challenging all those benefits that we have enjoyed throughout our lives. It would also entail questioning our ways, interactions, and behaviors towards people of color. An acknowledgment of racism in Mexico also calls for a deconstruction of our beloved, but toxic nationalism. López and Gutiérrez (2015) describe nationalism in the following way:

> Nationalism is a doctrine that proposes the autonomous, self-determined development of a defined community according to external, precise and homogeneous characteristics...Nationalism demands the concentration of political and economic decisions, elections, of ideological and cultural models. (para. 5)

Mexicans take these aspects of nationalism seriously—it is an ingrained sentiment among us. After the Mexican Revolution, nationalism became a unifying strategy in which politicians and authority figures attempted to shape the national identity—an identity which all Mexicans were supposed to fit (Ortíz & García, 2017). For instance, Rodríguez (2005) discusses how José Vasconcelos, also known as *the cultural caudillo* [the cultural leader] of the Mexican Revolution, talked about how *superior races* would gain control over those who he often described as the *weaker, uglier and inferior* people (referring specifically to People of Color, particularly Black and Indigenous people). Vasconcelos thought that by the mixture of European, Indigenous and Black blood, People of Color would improve their quality of life, as the Caucasian and European influences would enhance their opportunities to achieve an "ethnic improvement" (Vasconcelos, 1958, p. 933). Rodríguez (2005) critiques Vasconcelos' views of mestizaje, as within *La raza cósmica* [The cosmic race], which although published in 1958 is still considered one of the most iconic pieces of Mexican literature, and has informed our perception of Mexican history and identity. Specifically, Rodríguez points to the problematic way in which Vasconcelos makes anti-black and anti-Indigenous remarks and glorifies the powerful result that would emerge from the mixture of European, Indigenous and Black blood. Vasconcelos often highlighted how he allegedly did not glorified whiteness, but the end outcome of racial mixture, mestizaje, yet he often portrayed People of Color as incompetent, naturally oppressed, lazy, and weak. Rodríguez (2005) refutes the idea that *la raza* [Mexican race] would be a perfect combination of indigeneity and whiteness, and therefore would be superior and stronger.

Our nationalism goes hand in hand with forms of oppression such as racism and xenophobia, because our nationalism is built on the basis of whiteness. Yankelevich (2017) addresses the ingrained idea of unification regarding the argument about who can be Mexican and who cannot. Yankelevich asserts: "Being mestizo is the only way of being genuinely Mexican" (p. 130). From an early age, we learn that *all* of us are Mexican—the same—there is no diversity or differences between us. We *all* share a past that includes colonization and violence at the hands of the Spanish conquerors. Everyone is invited to claim this narrative of colonization, as though it was a phenomenon that affected every individual in Mexico equally. Yet, we are rarely encouraged to explore our various privileges and acknowledge the existent diversity within the Mexican population. Within this narrative, the experiences of several groups are immediately disregarded, specifically African Mexicans and Indigenous groups.

Homogenizing the nation does not foster a climate of equity and unity among Mexicans. Instead, we learn that only some of us can be considered Mexican and that *la patria* is the most important thing in the world. We fail to critique the principles behind the national festivities and the traditions that have pushed People of Color to the margins. This homogenization only benefits some of us and gives us the power of disenfranchising Communities of Color and Indigenous people. This serves to disregard a history of continuous oppression and xenophobia towards Asian communities, Central Americans, and furthers the erasure of African Mexicans, immigrants, and refugees from non-European countries.

1   Xenophobia *en Nuestra Casa*

After Porfirio Diaz's dictatorship and the end of Mexican Revolution, Mexico was in the process of reconstructing its identity. In order to create a collective sense of who *we* are, Mexico had to create an imagery of how *we* should look; how *we* behave, and what traditions and values *we* share as a group (Castro, 2015). Nationalism in Mexico is toxic as it does more than foster a sense of pride in being Mexican—it maintains racist and xenophobic attitudes towards Mexicans who do not easily fit our ideas of who Mexicans are—White or white-passing, a mixture of Spanish and Indigenous blood, which is what Vasconcelos portrayed in his work. This type of discrimination has a large scope, as we are also violent towards immigrants and refugees, especially if they are individuals of Color.

For years, Central Americans have been segregated and attacked in Mexican territory. Mexican border patrol authorities consistently marginalize Central American immigrants by exercising many types of violence, which is protected by faulty policymaking and protocols (Rico, 2016). However, Mexican society in general does its share of perpetuating such marginalization and keeping the xenophobia alive. Segregation has occurred across different spaces, and we are all involved in the perpetration of such manifestations of xenophobia and discrimination. Using so-called humor, we have normalized hate and stereotyping toward Central American people. We have labels for every country and highlight elements in which they are doing worse than us. We fail to challenge our media when it portrays the vulnerability of Central American countries as a joke. We also portray their citizens as unintelligent, not-beautiful, and non-human. Perhaps the reason we keep such rhetoric alive is because it allows us to assume superiority over Central American countries. Mexico has abused Central America in different ways throughout its policy, but it has also done so by failing to challenge prejudices and discrimination that emerge from our ingrained nationalism.

2 Ethnocentrism and Anti-Indigeneity

In elementary school, we studied the Tarahumara culture, as it was a part of the mandatory curriculum to learn about the different cultures within our state—Chihuahua. Because our education was rooted in Catholicism, Tarahumara culture was often addressed in a condescending or judgmental way. For instance, our teacher once pointed out how Tarahumaras did not have a close relationship with God, as we did, suggesting they needed to be educated in Catholicism as well. At the same time, we would be reminded that Tarahumaras are part of our culture and the richness of Chihuahua. The teacher's common narrative addressed them as elements that gave folklore and spice to our state, instead of highlighting the problematic issues of marginalization, and how we kept displacing them from their land.

We went to a museum to learn about the traditions of the Tarahumaras. Our teacher would address the traditions as non-valid and primitive. *"Las mujeres le avientan piedras a los hombres en los pies, luego ellas les ofrecen lavarles la ropa, que chistoso no?* [Tarahumara women throw little pebbles to men's feet, then they offer to wash their clothes. That is funny, isn't it?]" From such a problematic statement, and many other violent and anti-Indigenous teachings, we began our journey of entitlement, white supremacy, and Catholic superiority. We all learned to perceive Indigenous communities, their art, and language diversity as an experience of tourism. It was considered part of our heritage, something that we professed to respect and claimed whenever it was convenient or appropriate for us.

We were taught that we could admire and appropriate Indigenous blood whenever it suited us. *Look at the art they make. Wow! The richness and the colors, the flavors, and smell of the food Indigenous women cook in the main plaza. Let's go visit and dip in their culture for a couple of hours.* Then we would go back to our homes without deep learning or understanding, without a sense of responsibility for the oppression that these communities endure. Not only was I neglecting the relevance of experiences of Mexican People of Color and Indigenous communities, I learned to take from them. Internalizing capitalist narratives, non-Indigenous Mexicans often claim multiculturalism and claim respect towards indigeneity when we purchase Indigenous peoples' art or products; when we share a post on Facebook; perform other acts that are far from being transgressive or transformative. Yet, we will normalize their ongoing marginalization. Luz Elena Govea's case illustrates the exclusionary narrative towards Indigenous communities. Ms. Govea, is a Mexican deputy who also served as the local President of the Human Rights Commission in León Guanajuato, in 2016 addressed a group of Indigenous people who were asking her as the representative of local Human Rights Commission for support, as they had been harassed by officers in León Guanajuato. These workers were asking for respect and freedom to sell their products, as well as for better job opportunities. Her response:

> I say this with all due respect: when you ask for a job you need to take into consideration your aptitudes…I cannot imagine Indigenous women in a factory, cleaning a building or working behind a desk. I picture them in their homes making art. Working for their Indigenous communities… Let's consider that for the work you are asking for because if you abandon your land and traditions, us, the Mexican people will lack roots. Think about it when you want to envision a future. (Espinosa, 2016, para. 6)

Govea, at one point, compared her life to the lives of people in Indigenous communities, claiming that we all must work hard from our own places to make

Mexico a better country for everyone. Such comparison failed to acknowledge her own advantages as a non-Indigenous woman who occupied a powerful position. Throughout her narrative, Govea indicates this community is where *they*, as Indigenous people, should be, highlighting how Indigenous people's identity is critical for *our* country. She only addressed collectiveness when it was convenient for non-Indigenous people. This part of the narrative pertained to "everyone's roots and traditions," which selectively included indigeneity. After these remarks, Govea was removed from her position, yet what she had said reflects and reinforces anti-indigeneity.

As much as we would like to separate ourselves from what Govea has said, most Mexicans—particularly white and non-Indigenous Mexicans—have enacted the core ideas of her rhetoric. Although not all of us are public figures with a camera pointing at us at all times, most of us have disrespected indigeneity. We have portrayed it as an *exotic* trait of *our* Mexican identity, but we have failed to create and foster opportunities for equity and justice. Others have gone further using indigeneity as a joke to point out ignorance, lack of intelligence, and lack of familiarity with technology.

One example of how we demean indigeneity is our use of the word "*indio.*" It is often used to refer to someone who is not good with technology, does not have money, doesn't speak or understand English, and who does not dress well. It is also used overall to describe someone who is dark-skinned and poor. I have heard this expression countless times. People jokingly say; "*No seas indio* [don't be indio], *here is the power button.*" Indigenous memes were and still are a trend, the Nahuatl tongue has been reduced to a joke, where pictures of Indigenous women with their braided hair *laugh in Nahuatl* and every word ends with "tl." It is similar to the cliché about translating words from English to Spanish: when in doubt you should only write an "o" at the end. Why are these jokes still allowed and so well received by society? Are we really independent from colonization? What are the consequences of these so-called innocent jokes?

Anti-indigeneity jokes have reinforced a misleading perception of Indigenous communities as ignorant and childlike. Therefore, we have designated them a place of second- and third-class citizens. They live in the margins of every state in Mexico, bargaining their artwork and being arrested by the police for selling their products in public spaces. Women are beaten down, and children are denied education. How many of our assumptions of incompetence have been perpetuating these faulty policies and the lack of social security and enforcement of human rights?

> On this context, it is understood that the historical tendencies of economic exploitation and political control of Indigenous populations are

> possible because discrimination is justified in the context of daily interactions, which comprises structural racism, understood as a setting of social conditions that favor the negative qualification and the discrimination towards certain groups in a society. (Navarro, 2007, p. 109)

Not long ago, Rosalinda Guadalajara—an activist and representative of the Tarahumara community in Ciudad Juárez—was denied entrance to a very famous bar in Downtown Ciudad Juarez. Figueroa (2016) reports that the guards denied her the entry because of her identity and, as the bar claims, because of the shoes she was wearing. The guards at the entrance told her that they reserved their right of admission and that she was not allowed in, as the bar does not allow solicitors. The incident was recorded by Rosalinda's friends, and they were able to sue the bar. As a result, the bar ended up paying a fine for their discriminatory actions. However, in Mexico holding bars and establishments accountable for discrimination is not a common scenario.

Tarahumaras in Ciudad Juarez are abused and discriminated against on a continuous basis. Xenophobia and racism get a free pass in Mexico, through policies such as "we reserve the right to refuse entry." This policy marginalizes People of Color and vulnerable populations exclusively. I, as most White Mexicans, can enter any local establishment. I will never be questioned or followed around. My integrity will not be questioned and exposed like Rosalinda's. I will definitely not be immediately shut down. I will not be asked to leave a place because of the color of my skin, the way I speak, or the clothes I am wearing. All non-Indigenous Mexicans, including me, have contributed to the marginalization and erasure of Indigenous groups across the country. Our culture teaches us that they are part of our roots and heritage. We learn through curriculum and classroom rhetoric that Indigenous communities are a token or a charm for "Mexican folklore and identity." We are rarely encouraged to respect and contribute to removing barriers for these communities.

3 Humor and Media: Time for Accountability

> Cultural racism—the cultural images and messages that affirm the assumed superiority of Whiteness and the assumed inferiority of people of color—is like smog in the air. Sometimes it is so tick it is visible, other times is less apparent, but if we live in a smoggy place, how can we avoid breathing the air? (Tatum, 2013, p. 65)

Mexican humor, as popularly described, is rather peculiar, unique, and irreverent. All of these qualities are often stated as positive. In reference to the day of the death—an Indigenous tradition that all Mexicans have claimed as our own—we often say: *"Los Mexicanos nos reímos hasta de la muerte"* [Mexicans laugh at everything, even death]. A curious fact, we don't. At least in my family, we have no idea as to how to deal with loss. We are rarely taught how to let go of our loved ones. Even so, we say we find everything funny. We even say this about death, as if this allowed us to make fun of everything and everyone without the need for accountability, because "we laugh at ourselves first."

People in Mexico would even describe humor and comedy as a necessary coping mechanism for *everyone* to survive and make our lives and problems more bearable. I enjoy comedy and the humor engrained in pop culture. It was not until recently that I started to question the media that I have been consuming. Although there are stereotypical portrayals of Mexican people and People of Color around the world, none of these portrayals jeopardize my positionality. None of them threaten the power I hold as a cisgender White Mexican who is also documented. For those of us who are not affected by racist depictions in comedy, it is easy and comfortable to disregard—and even engage in such rhetoric—and move on with our days. This go-to move makes us highly responsible for bigoted depictions of people of color throughout the Mexican media.

In Mexico, it is common to constantly reaffirm hierarchies of power through a marginalizing rhetoric disguised as having *a sense of humor*. Laughing at other people's expense is common in Mexican humor, as long as we claim that we "we laugh at ourselves as well." We do not acknowledge that laughing at ourselves does not compromise our position of power or the way we are portrayed within society. We highlight the differences we have with other cultures and ridicule the *others*—those who are not part of a heteronormative, white, and Catholic-centered culture. We have jokes and nicknames for all vulnerable and marginalized populations and, because we hold power it is easy and comfortable for us to repeat and not challenge the narrative that diminishes the experiences of non-Catholic, non-white, and non-heterosexual individuals.

As discussed by De-Llano (2016), racism is a problem that pertains to the entire Mexican population—there is an interiorized and historical rejection toward Indigenous blood. How are these rejections still allowed? They are part of our daily conversations, exchanges, and jokes, which contribute to a harmful normalization of discourse. As stated by Navarrete (2016), "Mexican racism has a private and mocking aspect, in addition to its open and public forms" (p. 5). Mockery and *humor* allow racism and xenophobia, as long as they come in the form of a joke or a comment that was not supposed to *offend* anyone. It has become a habit of us, in Mexico, to avoid confrontation and accountability when being called out on our racist remarks. We get defensive and say that we were *only joking*—meaning, as long as a person of color is not around to hear me, I can get away with my comment because I was not hurting anyone (Navarrete, 2016). Again, *ojos que no ven, corazón que no siente*. This kind of *joking* relieves us from the responsibility of the inequitable conditions of our country for People of Color. We act as if our rhetoric and words were not powerful enough to depict individuals of Color as powerless and ignorant, because we are not the ones who are suffering the consequences of such portrayals.

4   The Influence of Media: Present and Past

Most millennials in Mexico can probably nostalgically remember the lullabies of Francisco Gabilondo Soler, aka Cri-Cri™ (1907–1990), which shows how relevant he has been for the Mexican musical scene. A famous Mexican singer, Gabilondo Soler wrote and sang songs for children. The characters of these songs have remained very much alive, as the songs have been passed on from one generation to the next one. Our parents and grandparents grew up listening to these songs, internalizing the stories of different characters that enriched their childhoods. Cri-Cri™ is such a strong influence on Mexican music, that his songs were transmitted from one generation to another one. This is especially the case in middle- and higher-class families, who had access to purchasing his music.

Roppolo (2013) reflects on the damage that cartoonish depictions have upon Native people in the United States, describing such a portrayal as "so ingrained in the American consciousness that is invisible" (p. 73). A similar phenomenon occurs in Mexico with depictions and portrayal of people of color, especially Black people. Listening to the stories in the form of songs allowed Mexican children to create stereotypes of certain groups of people. I am writing these lines knowing that some Mexican readers will instantly feel triggered and hurt, as I am *disturbing* our childhood memories. As I was doing my research for this chapter, I looked up Cri-Cri's™ songs online and listened carefully to the lyrics, so that I could be thorough in my analysis of his songs for this portion of the chapter. As I went through the comment section of each video, I noticed a minority of people commenting on the racist remarks present in some of Gabilondo Soler's lyrics. Most internet users were conflicted by the comments accusing Gabilondo Soler of using racist lyrics, stating that these songs were part of their childhood. They talked about how the songs brought them good memories—how dare we point out their flaws and attempt to ruin such memories.

A couple of these songs portray Black people as incompetent, as entertainers, and/or as individuals who are discontent with their skin color (Cepeda, 2018). Gabilondo Soler's lyrics include the n-word, which in Spanish some will argue that it is the literal translation of the word Black. However, the word is used in diminutive and portrays African and Black characters as rude, disrespectful, and untrustworthy. Other disrespectful labels were also used. There is a song that talks about a Black child whose name is "*Sandía*" [watermelon]. The song is about a little boy who is a loud, disrespectful, and rude. He curses the whole day and the song declares that he deserves to be disciplined with a stick by his aunt. This song is problematic for many reasons, beginning with the character's name and depiction. As Black (2014) explains, associating Black people with watermelon is highly racist and problematic, which most Mexicans continue to ignore and/or refuse to acknowledge.

> The stereotype that African Americans are excessively fond of watermelon emerged for a specific historical reason and served a specific political purpose. The trope came into full force when slaves won their emancipation during the Civil War. Free black people grew, ate, and sold watermelons, and in doing so made the fruit a symbol of their freedom. Southern whites, threatened by black's newfound freedom, responded by making the fruit a symbol of black people's perceived uncleanliness, laziness, childishness, and unwanted public presence. This racist trope then exploded in American popular culture, becoming so pervasive that its historical origin became obscure. (para. 3)

Another song talks about a wind-up toy that is a little Black man made of metal. The toy tap dances and entertains children. At one point in this song, Gabilondo Soler depicts the personality of the main character as lazy, warning listeners that the wind-up toy sometimes misbehaves. León (2016) argues that this song reinforces the bigoted stereotypes of Black people and Afro Latinx individuals such as a supposed willingness to dance in order to entertain other people.

Media representation greatly influences our perception towards diverse groups. Thus, Giménez (1996) argues that a consequence of an ongoing derogatory rhetoric towards vulnerable populations is the internalization of stigmas experienced by individuals regarding racial differences, sexual diversity, disabilities, and culture. Here we have a man considered a *national treasure*, a White Mexican who wrote many fables and memorable stories about animals, inanimate objects, and dolls. Gabilondo Soler made children happy for generations. Yet he has a very problematic side, which because of our nostalgia, we refuse to challenge.

Mr. Gabilondo Soler influenced the mindset of many Mexicans for generations—so much so, that his songs continue to be played in schools on a regular basis. The songs that depict racial stereotypes towards African, African American, and Chinese people are still used in schools for *pedagogical* purposes. Mother's Day is usually a time when most elementary classrooms prepare a dancing and singing number for the students' mothers. As part of these celebrations, Gabilondo Soler's songs have been performed by children, who are often wearing blackface (León, 2016). As I did my research, I found many comments from people nostalgically recalling dancing to one of these songs either dressed and characterized as a Chinese or a Black person in school. For years, blackface has not only allowed, but often encouraged/required by the schools. Therefore, is not surprising to me that after all these years, we continue to normalize racist remarks and even claim them as part of our educational formation and early childhood memories.

The time for accountability is now. Francisco Gabilondo Soler has passed away, but his influence remains culturally relevant in Mexico. There have been more conversations, studies, and discussions regarding racism being a critical issue in the country. However, we keep failing to identify, challenge, and even limit media elements that are harmful, toxic and excluding. We would rather prioritize our nationalist pride and white supremacist views. We have refused to be critical of the media rather than problematizing the complexities of these media images. Most importantly, we have continued to utilize controversial media, such as these songs and stories as educational tools. What are we replicating by doing this?

Mexican media has evolved slowly. The content that is produced in, and represents, Mexico is usually racially biased. As a White-passing Mexican, I've never had an issue finding positive representation of people who look like me in media or literature. Private schools, travel agencies, and real estate brokers, for instance, use White people to market their products. Everything that is aspirational or tries to sell us the idea of wellness, affluence, and high quality goods and services revolve around whiteness (Navarrete, 2016).

The content produced by Mexican media—soap operas, movies, television series, and musical and theater productions—centralize the experiences of White Mexicans, who are usually wealthy. Indigenous people continue to be portrayed as the loving and faithful servants who are there for the rich families at all times. They are depicted as if they were *part of the family*, but are still forced to cater to the needs of their employers. Black and Afro Latinx are never portrayed in these stories. In the rare instance that there is a black character, their story revolves around their blackness as a comedic opportunity and/or something problematic and which causes discomfort to the white characters.

Media does not cause but reinforces white supremacy, and such reinforcement has allowed Mexican society to normalize discrimination and racism throughout the years. Such normalization does not stay in the home. We can see it throughout policy. We can see it materialized in the last INEGI study with regard to discrimination based on skin tone. I do not visualize Mexican media changing soon. Mexican media will not change until we dare to dismantle our racism and learn to identify it from an early age. It is then that we will be ready to challenge the content that is presented to us. As consumers, we must identify racist remarks within our lives. We must recognize problematic rhetoric and behaviors that perpetuate an inequitable climate that negatively affects People of Color in our country.

5 Our Education

In Mexico, part of our almost nonexistent accountability lies in how we have been educated. We have learned by example and in theory that there is nothing we should apologize for, particularly when talking about race. We have learned to justify our racism towards People of Color by saying that the United States enacts racism towards Mexico; therefore, we feel entitled to do the same thing to other marginalized groups. And we think that we shouldn't be called out on it. We never recognize our privileges, where they come from, and how have we used them to contribute to different forms of oppression, such as racism. I didn't recognize or call out these behaviors when I was younger, and I certainly could have addressed issues of classism and racism with my students at the private schools where I taught in Mexico.

Back then, I did not know how to handle those topics, because I myself had not gone through that process. In one of the private schools I worked at, most children were upper class. Their parents drove brand new cars, and we as teachers were constantly reminded how important it was to treat them well. We were supervised in our interactions with these families, who had *important* last names. This made the work environment very tense and uncomfortable. I saw it as normal as within my mindset at the time; these people were *important*. Most of the children were White, and a minority were Children of Color. Almost all of my students came from wealthy, privileged families. When comparing this experience to my time teaching in the public schools, where most of my students were Children of Color, I do not recall anyone supervising my work closely. I do not remember anyone implying that I should be *careful* when addressing the families. Careful, in this context meaning being overly respectful and compliant with any request they would make for their children's education.

On a superficial and obvious level, this issue can be interpreted as classism. Private schools receive more income; therefore, rich children get better services than low-income and poor children at the private schools. However, racism is a component as well. The majority of children who were treated better were White. White children had access to resources and a skin color that is represented throughout the media as the standard of beauty and intelligence. These White children also received a better education, and their parents were entitled to participate actively in their learning process. Every time I taught children, I was an enthusiast teacher and did my best to provide my students with the best learning experience possible. At the same time, my teaching included unchallenged biases. For instance, being in the public schools, either in my short time teaching or when I volunteered, I knew that the resources were scarce. I saw this as normal—as something to be expected. I would bring materials from home without challenging the basis of scarcity for these kids. I had very few interactions with their parents, because most of them worked two jobs or more. Some of the children walked from home to school by themselves every day, which increased their vulnerability. All of these things, I ignorantly took to be normal circumstances for my students.

Being privileged and not checking my own power represents a missed opportunity of being a better teacher for my students—to enact accountability and to teach them how to do the same. Although I only served in the public schools for a short period of time before beginning my graduate program. I can see now how I could have done things differently. I wonder how many times I enacted willful ignorance and whether my lack of consciousness hurt my students' education during the time it was my responsibility. Time is something that we cannot get back. Fortunately, when willing to improve, time can potentially give us experience and the opportunity to reflect on and improve our praxis.

My skills in addressing social justice and racism were very limited in both public and private school environments, mostly because I had not challenged myself and my own biases in these settings. How would I expect my students to be mindful of their words and the consequences of their narratives and behaviors if I was not paying close attention to my own? Many of us are privileged enough that we get to learn about oppression through literature in graduate school, for example. However, even when we become aware of our privileges, there is resistance toward accountability and introspection.

We do have superficial discussions about socioeconomic disparities, racism, discrimination and other issues, yet the depth of these conversations is not profound because there is no accountability. In such circumstances, it is easier to be self-congratulatory and give ourselves a pat on the back for not using the n-word, or not being vocal in speaking against indigeneity and People of Color. In Mexico, there have been several historical moments that illustrate how racism and xenophobia have been a problem for centuries.

As a country that claims to prioritize education, we have done a poor job addressing issues from our past throughout history lessons and curriculum. Rodríguez (2005) goes back to the Conquest period when Mexico was named Nueva España, during which a hierarchic order based on whiteness prevailed. Such order implied that humanity was only a given for those who were European or passed as white. Those who were African and Indigenous were not considered human beings. Indigenous people were even referred to as "cuerpo sin razón" [purposeless body] (Rodríguez, 2005, p. 198).

Rodriguez (2005) also illustrates how People of Color in Mexico have been historically marginalized. This is particularly visible during the most significant civil wars in Mexico, such as the Mexican War of Independence and the Mexican Revolution. For instance, in 1857, all mention of diversity was erased from policy instead of reformulated. A nationalist model was being put into place, a model in which all Mexicans would fit.

A post-revolutionary Mexican identity was being created for everyone in Mexico to adopt. Castro (2015) discusses how powerful post-revolutionary groups in Mexico sought a national unification through a narrative which legitimized what meant to be Mexican. Such values dictated that Mexico was mostly made up of mestizo Mexicans. This mono-ethnic claim continues to prevail in Mexican society, erasing the existence and experiences of non-Mestizo groups in this country (Sotelo, 2015) and African ancestry and presence. Yankelevich (2017) highlights how during post-revolutionary times, being mestizo was the only valid way of identifying oneself as Mexican. Moreover, our education has led us to think that *mestizaje*, particularly when it closely resembles whiteness, is one of the things that makes us Mexican. This allows us to have the best of both worlds—Indigenous and European. Therefore, the argument is: *We are all equal. We are all the same. We do not perpetuate discrimination on the basis of race.* As non-Black and non-Indigenous Mexicans, we carry these exclusionary and white supremacist ideologies with us in contemporary times. A trip through Mexico includes not only a fun and enriching tourist experience, but the realization that the Indigenous communities remain living on the margins of society. At the same time, the Mexican mestizo, particularly the one who more closely approximates whiteness, dominates the spheres of power in the country.

"El que no conoce su historia, está condenado a repetirla" [Those who don't know their history are doomed to repeat it]. A teacher would use these words, drawn from the Aushwitz concentration camp, not as an opening line to learn about the genocide and racist history of our country, but as a warning for us Mexican citizens to defend our nation to avoid colonization once again. I do, however, find relevance in these words. I do not think that we have reached a

point where we know the uncomfortable parts of our history. Therefore, we keep repeating the same patterns. We keep repeating a narrative about how *we* are all products of a violent colonization, without stopping to reflect upon our own identities and how we colonize others. Furthermore, we feel comfortable with our portrayal as victims—including ourselves and our ancestors in the colonized Indigenous discussion whenever it is convenient, and quickly denying any indigeneity or Indigenous roots when it is not.

Contemporary and post-revolutionary nationalism in Mexico has harmed so many cultures. Yet, we have made very little effort to challenge it. I do not remember history lessons in which we learned about the concentration camps for the Japanese population in Mexico during Avila Camacho's administration (1940–1946). According to Peddie (2006), Mexican history has kept secrets out of the general curriculum. This includes the marginalization and forced grouping of Japanese communities in Mexico in 1942. He further explains: "The Japanese colony endured the phenomenon of being 'convicted on the basis of suspicion' and were judged solely for belonging, current or previously, to an 'enemy nation'" (Peddie, 2006, p. 94). Japanese people were stripped of their property by the Mexican authorities and removed from the borders and coasts of Mexico.

How does that unacknowledged past affect us in the present? Garduño (2016) specifically discusses the prejudice, xenophobia, and racism that occurs in Northern Baja California—the state which has the most cultural diversity in Mexico. This state claims to embrace diversity and multiple cultures, yet the minority groups that do not blend with whiteness continue to face ongoing discrimination. Garduño's example should highlight the importance of including Mexico's history of segregation in the curriculum so that those patterns of racism can be analyzed and dismantled. Racism against the Japanese community did not continue in the same way after Pearl Harbor. However, anti-Asian attitudes, jokes, and behaviors continue to exist in Mexico on a daily basis.

CHAPTER 5

Ableism

> Much of the public world is also structured as though everyone were physically strong, as though all bodies were shaped the same, as though everyone could walk, hear, and see well, as though everyone could work and play at a pace that is not compatible with any kind of illness or pain, as though no one were ever dizzy or incontinent or simply needed to sit or lie down.
>
> WENDELL (2013, pp. 482–483)

∴

About 6% of the Mexican population are identified as having a disability (INEGI, 2015). This percentage does not include the learning disabilities that have not been diagnosed due to a faulty assessment system. Mexico has a long way to go in terms of creating spaces, narratives, and representations that favors people with disabilities (ENADIS, 2011; Guevara & González, 2012; Guajardo, 2009). Therefore, I cannot talk about deconstructing privilege without addressing ableism in Mexico. Ableism is a form of discrimination from able-bodied or non-disabled people towards individuals with disabilities.

When I was in elementary school, I had special educational needs due to a medication I was taking to control multiple epilepsy seizures. My medication made me lethargic, sleepy, and distracted all the time. I lost a lot of weight and had a very difficult time focusing in school—especially in subjects that were challenging for me, such as Math. I remember my mother being apologetic to my teachers, explaining why I might take a little bit more time than other children to master the curriculum and pay attention in class. A couple of my teachers used my mother's explanations against me violently, embarrassing me in front of the whole class. My English teacher once mocked me for spacing out. She stood up in front of the whole class and mimicked my faces as I stared toward nothing in one of my periods of absence—a result of the medication I was taking. Of course, the whole class found the teacher's skit hilarious and mocked me for what felt like forever.

McEvoy (2005) states that "The threat of harm in bullying by teachers tends to be nonphysical, but nevertheless pervasive and powerful" (p. 3). The most common way of attacking students is through humiliation. Teachers who bully carefully select those students who seem vulnerable, in their eyes—those students who will seldom fight back. Bully professors constantly express how the victim differs from the rest of the group in a negative manner (Sylvester, 2011). In this situation, the rest of the group—the majority—are identified as more capable, valued, and accepted. The rest of the group then, is allowed to mock and ridicule a target child, as they have seen that the teacher, who holds most of the power in classroom, has does so herself (McEvoy, 2005; Tronco, Ramirez, Baggini, & Cervantes, 2013).

My fifth-grade teacher said to me that my mother had given him permission to physically discipline me and yell at me for not paying attention. I surely believed this, as he was the teacher and his word was unquestionable. So, I always tried to remain on my best behavior. I was not good at school, but I was good at sitting down and staying quiet. This teacher was verbally abusive and enjoyed humiliating me and other low-performing children in front of the whole class. I once performed really well on a Spanish test, as my mother had helped me study for it. Most of the class did poorly on the test. The teacher pulled my exam first, before anyone else's, and showed my perfect score. I thought this was a moment of recognition, I was very proud of myself. My teacher was very upset and said, "Look, even López who is the dumbest in the class was able to score well, what happened to the rest of you?" I remember the feeling of disappointment, even though I had scored well. I remember the frustration with my brain and what felt like a lack of intelligence due to the medication, even though I had achieved a high score.

Because of my difficulties learning and achieving coordination, a doctor had told my mother that it would be good for me to engage in some type of extracurricular activity, such as dancing, gymnastics, or swimming. My mother thought that dancing was a great choice for me. Dancing is beautiful and many of the exercises that we did focused on coordination and equilibrium. If the dance teacher said left I would hop, jump, and spin toward the right. I would lose my balance quickly, and the teacher made the other girls repeat the whole routine because I constantly messed up.

My teacher was short of patience, and on a couple of occasions she said that I did not have a brain. She called me dumb and slow. She would roll her eyes at me and use other terms and body language to condescendingly explain the dance moves and routines to me, always making sure that I knew how unintelligent she perceived me. Once, she said in front of the whole group that she did not know where to put me in the dance recital, as I was not able to do anything right. I definitely was a lot of work for this teacher. However, she did not hesitate to communicate her frustrations, exercising her power and portraying me as unintelligent and worthless in front of the whole group, who learned to perceive me the same way. Because of my absolute lack of coordination, it was pretty obvious that I was not going to pursue a career in dance. Although I do understand her frustration and how I might have been a lot of work for her, the derogatory remarks were unnecessary and left a lasting impression on me.

All of my teachers had information regarding my condition. My teachers were not only reluctant to adjust their instruction to accommodate my needs, they used my symptoms and weaknesses to ridicule me in front of the other children. My special education needs were moderately different than those of other children, and they were technically easy to address; yet no action was taken.

My medical condition was not the most severe, and my special education needs were not the most complex. I was privileged enough to have a timely and accurate diagnosis, and my parents were able to articulate and communicate my condition to my teachers. Despite the diagnosis and the side effects of my medication, I was still able-bodied and had social skills that allowed me to communicate and establish bonds and relationships with peers. Regardless of knowing the effects and consequences of my condition, my teachers did not know how to adjust their instruction. They did not know how to foster a learning environment in which I would feel safe, and they definitely fell short of removing barriers for my learning.

Parents trust their children with teachers on a continual basis, especially in Mexico, where back then, teachers represented a strong figure of authority. Concerns about bullying tend to be focused on peer-to-peer relationships, oftentimes parents do not even consider the possibility of teachers bullying their children. My parents never considered the idea of my teachers being abusive and violent. This is only one example of violence in the classroom, and considering what happens in the country on a daily basis, a pretty mild one, grounded on a privileged background.

My experiences do not represent what ableism looks like for everyone who is discriminated against. Clearly, my conditions were not as severe as many children, who have permanent intellectual, learning and/or physical disabilities or debilitating diseases, that unlike the epilepsy episodes I experienced as a child, cannot be treated with medication. However, I narrate my experiences in school to illustrate a small portion of our failure to work with disabilities and special education needs, as ableism gets in the way. Take into account how all of my teachers were aware of my condition and the side effects of my medication, and they could not—or chose not to—use their power and agency to make learning possible for me, as well as they probably did for many other children. Now imagine the lack of agency for undiagnosed children who are simply neglected and perceived as unintelligent.

For a long time in Mexico, special education was not a service, but a place—which, by the way, not every disabled child had access to. Special education services used to be provided at separated facilities, away from general education and non-disabled children. Although the term inclusion has been recently added to policy, the needs of students with all kinds of disabilities continue to be neglected due to scarce resources, lack of qualified personnel, and institutional ableism (health and educational). Such lack of accessibility for children with disabilities and special education needs have a more harmful impact in those populations who do not have the income to access private services and throughout wealth, ensure that their children receive an appropriate education and medical treatment.

The failure of my teachers to meet my needs only makes me think about cases which were more complex and severe than mine. For example, I think about all those students who had my teachers and other teachers in different learning settings, and other students who probably had teachers with similar or worst approaches than mine. Although these experiences happened in the 1990s, Mexican collective perception toward disabilities and special education needs has not evolved much. There is still an urgent need to transform the collective consciousness of non-disabled and able-bodied individuals in Mexico, particularly within the educational spaces.

People in Mexico consistently use disability labels to point out incompetence and stupidity among non-disabled peers. *Retrasado* [r-word], *inválido* [invalid], *mongolito* [Mongolian in Mexico is a pejorative term often used to refer to those with Down Syndrome, such a term carries racist connotations], are some derogatory and/or outdated terms that are used to formally allude to a disability but are still being used as insults. Our *ablebodiedness* and cultural beliefs around the boundaries of humor give us a sense of entitlement over those with disabilities—we assume that we can appropriate these identities solely for the purpose of joking about them. Behind closed doors and in private conversations, many of our *cruel jokes* include ableist narrative, portraying people with disabilities as stupid, and childish and point out their struggles, physical traits, and the things they cannot do.

Humor can also be a toxic defense mechanism. We sometimes use it this way when facing our own ignorance or when we do not know what to do with ourselves and our biases, or as we encounter people with different abilities than our own. I've seen the discomfort on people's faces, the "What do I do?" question when a client with an intellectual disability comes through the door. Our education has taught us to selectively learn what we need and to pay attention to the things that are relatable to us. When someone says: "They could be your children"—only then do we humanize others, when there is a form to connect their endurances to our lives and experiences.

Respect for the disabled community is almost non-existent. Therefore, there is little collective consciousness about creating spaces which everyone, regardless of their physical abilities, are able to access. Intellectual, learning, and physical disabilities have been neglected in Mexico. One can confirm this statement by observing the infrastructure, which is designed by and for able bodied people (Wendell, 2013). In Ciudad Juarez, for instance, you can often see the wheel chair ramps blocked by vehicles. People continue to park in the parking spots that are designed for those who struggle or lack mobility. Our architecture and infrastructure are as faulty as our unwillingness to learn and remove obstacles for others. Further, the educational system keeps pushing individuals with disabilities to the margins, denying an appropriate education tailored to their needs.

Ableism does not always come in the form of negative portrayal through comments and humor or by blocking/impeding the mobility and transitions of people with disabilities. Formal schooling and generational values have done their part to contribute to this collective culture of ableism. You will encounter the *pobrecito* [poor thing] narrative, in which we try to portray ourselves as saviors—compassionate able-bodied individuals who see and validate the experiences of people with disabilities. Yet pity, too, is a form of oppression. Through the *poor thing* narrative, we enforce the idea of the superiority of able-bodied individuals. We construct a permanent principle of *being compassionate* and move on with our lives. There is no transformation in this. There are no lessons learned, much less a shift in power relationships or removal of barriers.

My lived experiences with epilepsy in no way exempt me from embodying ableism. Have I used my able-bodied privilege for making the spaces I occupy accessible for individuals with disabilities? Not as much as I should have. Not using derogatory terms towards people with disabilities or not parking in the handicap parking spot does not make you responsive and respectful towards the disabled community. "Challenging ableism truly requires that we recognize how this oppression is manifested on the individual, institutional, and cultural levels of engagement" (Peters, Castaneda, Hopkins, & McCants, 2013, p. 113). My understanding of disabilities came from a place of pity, the way we are taught in school and media. As I became educated and started reaching out to the information, resources, and literature, I began to understand my biases.

My own desire to study special education comes, in part, from the internalized ideology of *helping others*. My intentions to improve education were genuine. I was aware, to some extent, of the injustices that affected the lives of people with disabilities in Mexico. I wanted to provide appropriate resources for my special education students so that they may have the same opportunities as their able-bodied peers to learn and to thrive in school. However, throughout my undergraduate program, I rarely challenged my own my biases and ideologies regarding disabilities. I didn't consider how my belief of what *helping* meant or how it could harm or deprive my students from a more meaningful education. Such values initially permeated my work. At the beginning of my practicum, I thought that I would need to assist my students with physical mobility, as they transitioned from one classroom to the next. I thought that I had to be extra mindful in order to help them move between spaces, instead of acknowledging that they had mastered orientation and mobility for a very long time. My beginner mentality was not focused on learning the content of braille and teaching them literacy. I was too worried about how I could *help*, rather than how to accurately accommodate the curriculum and instruction for my students' needs so that I could *teach*.

After a couple of months in my practicum experience, I identified some issues related to my presumed *goodwill*, yet I could not name the phenomenon or articulate what those reflections meant to me. I would often get comments on what a wonderful job I was doing, and how "It takes a certain type of person" to do the work I was trying to learn. Such mentality, benevolent if you will, is also a challenge to overcome in Mexico. Thinking that only *special people*—who have good hearts and a lot of patience—can take on the endeavor of educating children with disabilities, contributes to the disempowerment of the disabled community.

We have reinforced the erroneous idea that it is not everyone's responsibility to remove barriers for people with disabilities to have opportunities to succeed without mobility and social barriers, and have a quality of life. We have become comfortable limiting our reflections to sentiments of pity toward everyone who isn't able-bodied. This does not involve any sort of transformative action on our part. Rather, we tend to enact complacently toward a society filled with barriers and gaps, which are imposed on those who are not able-bodied. Pity and the *pobrecito* rhetoric allows us to remain comfortable and maintain our power.

According to the National Survey of Discrimination in Mexico (ENADIS), seven out of every 10 Mexican citizens agreed that the human rights of individuals with disabilities are not honored in the country. My hope, as a future specialist in this area, is to educate the able-bodied. I aim to use my privilege to remove barriers. This work also entails for me to continue educating myself so that I recognize when I create barriers and obstacles for others through my attitudes, behaviors, and reluctance to challenge other's belittling narratives. For years, the services, adaptations and modifications tailored for the disabled community have been perceived as luxuries—something that may not even be used as *they are a minority*. Our collective consciousness must shift. Our power as able-bodied individuals has allowed us to be complacent, and these perceptions remain unchallenged. Therefore, we have collectively given a free pass to our government and our society to continue on with non-accessible infrastructure planning; a faulty educational system that continues to fail people with different abilities; and lousy policymaking that claims inclusion, but rarely accomplishes this goal.

CHAPTER 6

Towards a New Light

This book only begins to touch upon my understandings around problematic issues, behaviors, and structures that exist in Mexican society. Starting to unpack my own experiences and understandings of power and privilege has allowed me to identify the moments and ways in which I have engaged in problematic behaviors and the products, media, and *art* I have consumed uncritically. I have found that by recounting my experiences and reflecting upon certain anecdotes, I've been able to understand the moments in which my thoughts and behaviors have been problematic or complicit. I have also considered the situations in which I could have acted or intervened differently—perhaps in my praxis as a teacher, or during a conversation with close friends and family members. I do not expect every Mexican reader to relate to my experiences, I do hope that my reflections can help facilitate reflexivity and self-criticism for others.

The privilege that many White, heterosexual, able-bodied, middle-class, wealthy, and documented Mexicans in Mexico hold might seem evident to other people, who see Mexicans from the outside. That is not as easy when you are an insider who is also comfortable. My hope with this book is to encourage Mexicans to identify their/our own privileges, unpack them, and have an understanding of the problematic behaviors we support and engage in every day of our lives. How would our ingrained toxicity change if we stopped using attacks on foreigners, immigrants, Central American asylum seekers, documented and undocumented Mexican Americans in the United States, People of Color, and refugees who need to cross over our territory as ways to *defend la patria*? It would be interesting to witness what could happen with our country if we dared to shift our ideologies around humor and our constant need to degrade and minimize others to feel superior and powerful.

Reflecting critically upon my own education has not been an easy task, nor has it been easy to point out the ways in which machismo and conservative familial values have permeated my education. However, it is important to identify the ways in which my education has had many flaws and gaps, not only academically but ideologically. The most challenging part for me has been to understand why and how I have been reluctant to challenge the toxicity of my own ideologies.

I believe that the reconstruction of a respectful and socially just society begins with *cleaning our own home,* that is by thinking critically about our own values and whether those values have marginalized others. A transformation can occur by reaching out to experts and sources of information that allow us to gain more perspective than what we have learned thus far. I would like for folks in Mexico to think twice before saying, laughing at, or encouraging racist, xenophobic, or ableist jokes. I don't know about you, but I am craving smarter humor—clever comedy that does not involve disempowering vulnerable groups.

Some of us, due to our multiple privileged identities and ingrained entitlement, need to reach out to literacy and resources in order to learn how not to be toxic; how to stop being harmful; and to unlearn problematic values that have shaped our lives. It is our responsibility to educate ourselves. Vulnerable groups—the communities that we have constantly marginalized—do not have the obligation of explaining their humanity to us. I've heard many times, this rhetoric of people wanting the *other* to convince them about their worthiness, their value. We are so reluctant to give away our power and advantages. It is our own responsibility to educate ourselves, to reach out to resources, and hopefully to do better.

With that said, it is important to be mindful that those we have hurt are not forced to apologize to us or to forgive us for how we've hurt them. Our willingness to learn and do better—the work we do to improve ourselves—can only mean so much against the potential harm we have caused in the past. Vulnerable groups are not required to forgive and forget what we have done to them. This must be clear to us, as we will constantly find ourselves in positions that require for us to engage in acts of accountability. Challenging individuals around us, colleagues, family members, community leaders would be a good start.

References

Aboites, H. (2012). El derecho a la educación en México. Del liberalismo decimonónico al neoliberalismo del siglo XXI. *Revista Mexicana de Investigación Educativa, 7*(53), 361–389.

Adams, M. (2013). Classism. In M. Adams, W. Blumenfeld, C. R. Castaneda, M. L. Peters, & X. Zúniga (Eds.), *Readings for diversity and social justice* (pp. 141–156). New York, NY: Routledge.

África Fundación Sur. (2016). México reconoce a los afro-mexicanos en su nuevo censo. *Crónicas y Reportajes.* Retrieved June 2019, from http://www.africafundacion.org/spip.php?article25600

Alva, A. R. d. (2015). Los nuevos rostros de la desigualdad en el siglo XXI. *Revista Mexicana de Ciencias Políticas y Sociales, 60*(223), 265–285.

Applequist, J. (2014). Pinterest, gender reveal parties, and the binary: Reducing an impending arrival to 'pink' or 'blue.' *Pennsylvania Communication Annual, 70,* 51–665.

Balderas, O. (2017). *Papás ricos y niños bonitos: así se discrimina en algunas escuelas privadas de México.* Vice Operadores de la Discriminación. Retrieved April 23, 2019, from https://www.vice.com/es_latam/article/yw9d8g/papas-ricos-ninos-bonitos-discrimina-escuelas-privadas-mexico

Bartra, E. (1999). El movimiento feminista en México y su vínculo con la academia. *La Ventana, 1*(1–10), 214–234.

Bastilda, L., & Navarro, C. (2018). Violencia, impunidad y prejuicios: los crímenes del odio. *La Jornada del Campo. Agrosexualidades.* Retieved May 2019, from https://www.jornada.com.mx/2018/06/16/cam-violencia.html

Berlanga, G. M. (2015). The spectacle of violence in contemporary Mexico: From femicide to juvenicidio (young killing). *Athenea Digital. Revista de Pensamiento e Investigación Social, 15*(4), 105–128.

Bernal, L. R. (2018). Producción de discursos sobre sexualidad en la escuela y heteronormatividad: el caso de un profesor de Biología. *Revista de Colegio de San Luis, 8*(15), 269–290.

Black, W. (2014). How watermelons became a racist trope. *The Atlantic, 8.*

Blancarte, R. (2008). El por qué de un Estado laico. *Foro de Libertades Laicas, 12.* Retrieved August 23, 2018, from http://www.colectiva-cr.com/sites/default/files/Docs/publicaciones/Memorias%20FLL_version%20digital.PDF

Boivin, R. R. (2014). "Se podrían evitar muchas muertas." Discriminación, estigma y violencia contra minorías sexuales en México. *Sexualidad Salud y Sociedad-Revista Latinoamericana, 16,* 86–120.

Buck, S. A. (2001). El control de la natalidad y el día de la madre: política feminista y reaccionaria en México, 1922–1923. *Signos Históricos, 5,* 9–53.

Cano, G. (2013). Debates en torno al sufragio y la ciudadanía de las mujeres en México. *Estudios Sociologicos, XXXI*, 7–20.

Castañeda, C., & Zúñiga, Z. (2013). Racism. Introduction. In M. Adams, W. Blumenfeld, C. R. Castaneda, M. L. Peters, & X. Zúniga (Eds.), *Readings for diversity and social justice* (pp. 57–64). New York, NY: Routledge.

Castillo, S. C. (2014). Religión y política. *Alteridades, 24*, 153–160.

Castro, M. G. (2015). Identidad nacional y nacionalismo en México. *Sociológica México*. Retrieved December 4, 2017, from http://www.sociologicamexico.azc.uam.mx/index.php/Sociologica/article/view/773

Catalano, C., & Shlasko, D. (2013). Transgender oppression: Introduction. In M. Adams, W. Blumenfeld, C. R. Castaneda, M. L. Peters, & X. Zúniga (Eds.), *Readings for diversity and social justice* (pp. 425–431). New York, NY: Routledge.

Cech, E. A. (2017). Rugged meritocratists: The role of overt bias and the meritocratic ideology in Trump supporters' opposition to social justice efforts. *Socius, 3*. doi:10.1177/2378023117712395

Cepeda. (2018, May 1). *Cri-Cri el grillito cantor is beloved by Mexican children, but it has an unexamined problematic past*. Remezcla. Retrieved April 28, 2019, from https://remezcla.com/features/music/cri-cri-el-grilito-cantor-op-ed/

CNA. (2014, June 7). *Pope: Fear of the Lord an alarm reminding us of what's right*. Catholic News Agency. Retrieved June 6, 2018, from https://www.catholicnewsagency.com/news/pope-fear-of-the-lord-an-alarm-reminding-us-of-whats-right-48609

Coss, D., Coss, L., & Parra, J. C. V. (2018). La posibilidad de creencias religioso-regionales. Una aproximación desde el significado de la religión católica en el Occidente de México. *Revista Humanidades, 8*(1), 121–136.

De-la-Calle, L., & Rubio, L. (2010). *Clasemediero*. México D.F.: Felou.

de la Torre, R. (2016). Ser islámico en Guadalajara está en musulmán. *Espiral, 23*(65), 245–253.

de la Torre, R. (2018). Alianzas interreligiosas que retan la laicidad en México. *Revista Rupturas, 9*(1), 155–178.

De-Llano, P. (2016, June 30). ¿Es México Racista? *El Pais*.

D'Emilio, J., & Freedman, E. B. (2012). *Intimate Matters. A history of sexuality in America*. Chicago, IL: University of Chicago Press.

de la Rubia, J. M., & Basurto, S. R. (2016). Machismo, victimización y perpetración en mujeres y hombres mexicanos. *Estudios sobre las culturas contemporáneas, 22*(43), 37–66.

Despagne, B. C. (2015). Modernidad, colonialidad y discriminación en torno al aprendizaje del inglés en Puebla, México. *Trace México D.F., 68*, 59–80.

Dossier político. (2006, December 23). *La educación privada en México*. Retrieved April 23, 2018, from http://www.dossierpolitico.com/vernoticiasanteriores.php?artid=15616

REFERENCES

El Economista. (2011, May 24). Alcade se retracta de prohibir minifaldas en Sinaloa. *El Economista*. Retrieved February 24, 2018, from https://www.eleconomista.com.mx/estados/Alcalde-se-retracta-de-prohibir-minifaldas-en-Sinaloa-20110524-0098.html

El País. (2016, April 22). El feminicidio en Ciudad Juárez, la historia sin final. *El País*. Retrieved May 8, 2017, from https://elpais.com/internacional/2015/05/15/actualidad/1431653222_213789.html

Elenes, A. C. (2010). *Transforming borders: Chicana/o popular culture and pedagogy*. Lanham, MD: Lexington Books.

ENADIS. (2011, June). *Encuesta Nacional sobre la Discriminación en México. Resultados sobre las mujeres*. Consejo Nacional para Prevenir la Discriminación. Retrieved from https://www.conapred.org.mx/documentos_cedoc/Enadis-MUJERES-WEB_Accss.pdf

Englander, K., Yáñez, C., & Barney, X. (2012). Doing science within a culture of machismo and marianismo. *Journal of International Women's Studies, 13*(3), 65–85.

Espinosa, V. (2016, April 4). Relevan de comisión a diputada que aconsejó a indígenas "no dejar de vender sus nopalitos." *Proceso*. Retrieved August 15, 2018, from https://www.proceso.com.mx/437136/relevan-comision-a-diputada-dijo-a-indigenas-dejen-vender-sus-nopalitos

Espinosa-Hernández, G. (2015). Sexual behaviors in Mexico: The role of vlues and gender across adolescence. *Archives of Sexual Behavior, 44*(4), 895–902.

Faniko, K., Lorenzi-Cioldi, F., Ghisletta, P., Øyslebø, S., Sørensen, E. M., Shalsi, F., & Chipeaux, M. (2015). When meritocracy opposes a quota policy. In K. Fanico, F. Lorenzi-Cioldi, O. Sarrasin, & E. Mayor (Eds.), *Gender and Social Hierarchies: Perspectives from Social Psychology*. New York, NY: Routledge.

Figueroa, L. (2016, November 28). Kentucky Club in Juárez fined over discrimination. *El Paso Times*. Retrieved September 2, 2018, from https://www.elpasotimes.com/story/news/local/juarez/2016/11/28/kentucky-club-jurez-fined-over-discrimination/94571248/

Fuller, N. (1995). *Acerca de la polaridad marianismo machismo*. Bogota: Ediciones Unidades.

Garduño, E. (2016). La frontera norte de México: Campo de desplazamiento, interacción y disputa. *Frontera Norte, 28*(55), 131–151.

Gil-Romo, S. E., & Coria, S. D.-U. (2007). Estudios sobre alimentación y nutrición en México: una mirada a través del género. *Salud Pública de México, 49*(6), 445–453.

Giménez, G. (1996). La identidad social o el retorno del sujeto en sociología. *Identidad: análisis y teoría, simbolismo, sociedades complejas, nacionalismo y etnicidad*. México: III Coloquio Paul Kirchhoff.

González, J. H., & Ríos, A. A. (2017). Abstencionismo electoral y adscripción religiosa en México: apuntes para una agenda de investigación. *Estudios Políticos, 40*, 105–121.

Guajardo, R. E. (2009). Integration and inclusion of disabled students in Latin America and the Caribbean. *Revista Latinoamericana de Educación Inclusiva, 3*(1), 15–23.

Guevara, B. Y., & González, S. E. (2012). Las familias ante la discapacidad. *Revista Electrónica de Psicología Iztacala, 15*(13), 1023–1050.

Gutiérrez Gamboa, D. I., García, E. A. A., Winton, A., & Margaret, A. (2018). Mujeres transgénero trabajadoras sexuales en Chiapas: las violencias del proceso de construcción y reafirmación de su identidad de género. *Sociológica (México), 33*(94), 139–168.

Gómez-Peralta, H. (2007). La Iglesia católica en México como institución de derecha. *Revista Mexicana de Ciencias Políticas y Sociales, 49*(199), 63–78.

Grinde Jr., D. A. (2004). Taking the Indian out of the Indian: U.S. policies of ethnocide through education. *Wicazo SA Review, 19*, 25–32.

Hardiman, R., Jackson, B. W., & Griffin, P. (2013). Conceptual foundations. In M. Adams, W. Blumenfeld, C. R. Castaneda, M. L. Peters, & X. Zúniga (Eds.), *Readings for diversity and social justice* (pp. 26–35). New York, NY: Routledge.

Harro, B. (2013). The cycle of socialization. In M. Adams, W. Blumenfeld, C. R. Castaneda, M. L. Peters, & X. Zúniga (Eds.), *Readings for diversity and social justice* (pp. 45–56). New York, NY: Routledge.

hooks, b. (2010). *Where we stand: Class matters.* New York, NY: Routledge.

Incháustegui, T. R. (2014). Sociología política del feminicidio; algunas claves interpretativas a partir del caso mexicano. *Revista Sociedade e Estado, 29*(2), 373–400.

INEGI. (2011). *Instituto Nacional de Estadística y Geografía.* Retrieved January 17, 2017, from http://internet.contenidos.inegi.org.mx/contenidos/productos/prod_serv/contenidos/espanol/bvinegi/productos/estudios/sociodemografico/mujeresrural/2011/EUM/702825051266_1.pdf

INEGI. (2013a). *Instituto Nacional de Estadística y Geografía.* Retrieved April 3, 2017, from http://www.inegi.org.mx/inegi/contenidos/investigacion/Experimentales/Clase_media/doc/clase_media_resumen.pdf

INEGI. (2013b). *Cuantificando la clase media en México: un ejercicio exploratorio.* Retrieved April 19, 2018, from https://www.inegi.org.mx/contenidos/investigacion/cmedia/doc/cmedia_resumen.pdf

INEGI. (2015). *Estadisticas a proposito del dia mundial de las personas con discapacidad.* Retrieved April 15, 2017, from http://www.inegi.org.mx/saladeprensa/aproposito/2015/discapacidado.pdf

INEGI. (2017a). *Presenta INEGI, por vez primera, resultados sobre la movilidad social intergeneracional.* Retrieved October 10, 2017, from http://www.inegi.org.mx/saladeprensa/boletines/2017/mmsi/mmsi2017_06.pdf

INEGI. (2017b). *Presentan publicación sobre perfil de la población afrodescendiente en México.* Retrieved January 4, 2018, from http://www.inegi.org.mx/saladeprensa/boletines/2017/especiales/especiales2017_03_04.pdf

REFERENCES

Jeppesen, A. M. E. (2015). Dejar las lágrimas e ir hacia las acciones. La Frontera Norte, Ciudad Juárez y los feminicidios. *Sociedad y Discurso, 27*.

Jones, C. W. (2019). Racism and classism in Mexican advertising. In A. Olteanu, A. Stables, & D. Borţun (Eds.), *Meanings & Co.* (pp. 213–266). Cham: Springer.

Joshi, K. Y. (2006). *New roots in America's sacred ground* (pp. 118–114). New Brunswick, NJ: Rutgers University Press.

Kan, E. M. (2014). La dinámica de la pluralidad religiosa en México. *Estudios Teologicos, 54*(1), 53–68.

Labrie, D. (2018). *Intra-racial and ethnic othering among the Mexican-origin population in the Southwest*. Tucson, AZ: The University of Arizona.

Lamas, M. M., Tarrés, M. L., & Tuñon, E. (1995). Mexico building bridges: The growth of popular feminism in Mexico. *Trans Ellen Calmus*, 324–347.

Lechuga, J. M., Guerrero, M., & Ramírez, A. J. (2015). Educación y género, el largo proceso del rol de la mujer en la economía de México. *Investigación Cualitativa en Educación, 2*, 133–138.

León, C. V. M. (2016). Yo no me siento contigo. Educación y racismo en pueblos afromexicanos. *Diálogos sobre Educación. Temas actuales en investigación educativa, 7*(13), 1–17.

Lipsitz, G. (2013). The possessive investment in Whiteness. In M. Adams, W. Blumenfeld, C. R. Castaneda, M. L. Peters, & X. Zúniga (Eds.), *Readings for diversity and social justice* (pp. 77–86). New York, NY: Routledge.

López, R. G., & Gutiérrez, J. L. (2015). En torno a la redefinición del nacionalismo mexicano. *Sociológica México, 21*. Retrieved March 25, 2017, from http://www.sociologicamexico.azc.uam.mx/index.php/Sociologica/article/viewFile/776/749

Loza, J. (2015). La clase media, agencia y actor social de políticas públicas: Ciudadanía y derechos sociales. *Contextualizaciones Latinoamericanas, 4*(7), 1–12.

Lozano-Verduzco, I. (2017). *Efectos de la homofobia internalizada en la salud mental y sexual de hombres gay de la Ciudad de México*. Retrieved May 1, 2019, from http://cnegsr.salud.gob.mx/contenidos/descargas/GySenC/Volumen14_3/04_Efectos_de_la_hemofobia.pdf

Lugo, C. (1985). Machismo y violencia. *Nueva Sociedad, 78*, 40–47.

Mantsios, G. (2013). Class in America. In M. Adams, W. Blumenfeld, C. R. Castaneda, M. L. Peters, & X. Zúniga (Eds.), *Readings for diversity and social justice* (pp. 150–156). New York, NY: Routledge.

Martínez, L. F. M. (2015). La inequidad de género en el México moderno. *Entretextos, 7*(20). Retrieved April 2018, from https://reader.elsevier.com/reader/sd/pii/S0185191815721380?token=8A2D29206FAE9DA2603885E9BBBF5788675D83AC1C01F14F1F3E05EC717A62407545616FED03ED31E33E069CC3F7D6A7

Martínez, O. L. R. (2016). Masculinidad y vida conyugal en México. Cambios y persistencias. *GénEr♀♂ s, 18*(10), 79–104.

McEvoy, A. (2005, September 11–14). Teachers who bully students. Patterns and policy implications. In *Proceedings of Conference on Persistently Safe Schools*. Philadelphia, PA: Wittenberg University.

Medrano, A. B., Miranda, M. M., & Figueras, V. M. (2017). Violencia de pareja contra las mujeres en México: una mirada a la atención del sector salud desde una perspectiva interseccional. *Multidisciplinary Journal of Gender Studies, 6*(1), 1231–1262.

Moctezuma, N. D., Narro, R. J., & Orozco, H. L. (2013). Women in Mexico: Inequality, poverty and violence. *Revista Mexicana de Ciencias Políticas y sociales, 59*, 117–146. Retrieved from http://www.scielo.org.mx/pdf/rmcps/v59n220/v59n220a5.pdf

Monsivais, C. (1995). Ortodoxia y heterodoxia en las alcobas (Hacia una crónica de costumbres y creencias sexuales en Mexico). *Debate Feminista*, 183–210.

Moral, D. L., & Ramos, B. S. (2016). Machismo, victimización y perpetración en mujeres y hombres mexicanos. *Estudios sobre las Culturas Contemporáneas, 22*(43), 37–66.

Moreno, A. A. R. (2017). Nunca más un México sin nosotras. La participación de las mujeres en el proyecto político del Congreso Nacional Indígena. *Ecología Política*, 93–97.

Moreno Figueroa, M. G. (2016). El archivo del estudio del racismo en México. *Desacatos, 51*, 92–107.

Muskus, M., C. (2018). Los problemas con los conocidos eventos de "revelación de género" o "gender reveal." *Tribuna Feminista*. Retrieved May 2019, from https://tribunafeminista.elplural.com/2018/04/los-problemas-con-los-conocidos-eventos-de-revelacion-de-genero-o-gender-reveal/

National Network of the U.S. Immigration Policing Regime. (2010). Injustice for all: The rise of the U.S. Immigration Policing Regime. *Human Rights Community Action Network*. Retrieved June 2019, from http://www.racialequitytools.org/resourcefiles/nnir.pdf

Navarrete, F. (2016). *México racista: Una denuncia*. México City: Grijalbo.

Navarro, S. A. (2007). Los indígenas no hablan "bien" Defensores comunitarios, ciudadania étnica y retos ante el racismo estructural el México. *Culturales, 3*(4), 105–133.

Ortíz, E. M., & García, R. A. (2017). Confluencia migratoria en México: retos legales, administrativos y socioculturales de la nueva diversidad. *Procesos migratorios en el occidente de México*, 133–170.

Pacheco, V. (2016, August 6). *Diversidad sexual, el tabú del México conserbador*. Retrieved May 2017, from https://sipse.com/mexico/diversidad-sexual-tabu-mexico-conservador-libros-texto-sep-216638.html

Palomar, V. C., & Suarez, d. G. (2007). Los entretelones de la maternidad. A la luz de las mujeres filicidas. *Estudios Sociologicos*, 309–340.

Paz, O. (1993). *El laberinto de la soledad* (Vol. 346). Madrid: Cátedra.

REFERENCES

Peddie, F. (2006). Una presencia incómoda: La colonia japonesa de México durante la Segunda Guerra Mundial. *Estudios de Historia Moderna y Contemporánea de México, 32*, 73–101.

Peters, M. L., Castaneda, C. R., Hopkins, L. E., & McCants, A. (2013). Recognizing ableist beliefs and practices and taking action as an ally. In M. Adams, W. Blumenfeld, C. R. Castaneda, M. L. Peters, & X. Zúniga (Eds.), *Readings for diversity and social justice* (pp. 532–542). New York, NY: Routledge.

Pittelman, K., Resource Generation (2013). Deep thoughts about class privilege. Classism. In M. Adams, W. Blumenfeld, C. R. Castaneda, M. L. Peters, & X. Zúniga (Eds.), *Readings for diversity and social justice* (pp. 141–156). New York, NY: Routledge.

Proceso. (2014, September 20). "Las leyes, como las mujeres, se hicieron para violarlas": Exdiputado priista de Chiapas (L. Redaccion, Ed.). *Tendencias*. Retrieved November 23, 2017, from https://www.proceso.com.mx/382569/las-leyes-como-las-mujeres-se-hicieron-para-violarlas-exdiputado-priista-de-chiapas

Rico, I. V. (2016). Ser "el otro": Migración, xenofobia y derechos humanos en México contemporáneo. *Revista Semestral de El Colegio de Taxcala, 31*(71), 71–80.

Rodriguez, C. L., Rodriguez, M. A., & Ramirez, M. T. (2004). Design and psychometric properties of the sexual machism scale (EMS-Sexism-12). *SUMMA Psicologica UST, 7*(2), 35–44.

Rodriguez, M. J. C., Valdez, E. M. A., Ibáñez, S. E. D., Pérez, R. R., Montaño, A. H., & Salazar, J. Z. (2016). Creencias sobre estereotipos de género de jóvenes universitarios del norte de México. *Diversitas: Perspectivas en Psicología, 12*(2), 217–230.

Rodríguez, Z. L. (2005). Prejuicio y discriminación en el contexto político de México. *Estudios de Antropología Biológica, 12*(1), 195–221.

Roppolo, K. (2013). Symbolic racism, history, and reality. The real problem with Indian mascots. In M. Adams, W. Blumenfeld, C. R. Castaneda, M. L. Peters, & X. Zúniga (Eds.), *Readings for diversity and social justice* (pp. 73–77). New York, NY: Routledge.

Ruiz, I. (2015). "El diablo en el cuerpo:" Transfiguraciones contraexpresivas en torno a los feminicidios en Ciudad Juarez. *El Ornitorrinco Tachado. Revista de Artes Visuales*, 25–40.

Saraví, G. A. (2016). Reciprocal looks: Representations of inequality in Mexico. *Revista Mexicana de Sociología, 78*(3), 409–436.

Schmelkes, S. (2006, May 11). *La interculturalidad en la educación básica*. UNESCO, El curriculo a debate. Retrieved August 27, 2017, from http://www.socolpe.org/data/normalarmenia/BIBLIOGRAFIA/interculturalidad_educacion_basica_schmelkes.pdf

SEDESOL. (2013). *Gobierno de la República Mexicana*. Retrieved May 14, 2017, from http://www.sedesol.gob.mx/work/models/SEDESOL/Transparencia/DocumentosOficiales/Programa_Sectorial_Desarrollo_Social_2013_2018.pdf

Serano, J. (2013). Trans woman manifesto. In M. Adams, W. Blumenfeld, C. R. Castaneda, M. L. Peters, & X. Zúniga (Eds.), *Readings for diversity and social justice* (pp. 443–446). New York, NY: Routledge.

Schlosser, L. Z. (2003). Christian privilege: Breaking a sacred taboo. *Journal of Multicultural Counseling & Development, 31*, 195–210.

Shuck, N. C. (2008). Literatura de escritura femenina. *Revista Borradores, 8*(9), 1–10.

Sotelo, F. G. (2015). Nación y nacionalismo en México. *Sociológica México, 21*.

Sylvester, R. (2011). Teacher as a bully. Knowingly or unintentionally harming students. *The Delta Kappa Gamma Bulletin, 77*(22), 42–46.

Tapia, L. A., & Valenti, G. (2016). Desigualdad educativa y desigualdad social en México. Nuevas evidencias desde las primarias generales en los estados. *Perfiles Educativos, 38*(151), 32–54.

Tatum, B. D. (2013). Can we talk? In M. Adams, W. Blumenfeld, C. R. Castaneda, M. L. Peters, & X. Zúniga (Eds.), *Readings for diversity and social justice* (pp. 65–73). New York, NY: Routledge.

Taylor, E. (2013). Cisgender privilege: On the privileges of performing normative gender. In M. Adams, W. Blumenfeld, C. R. Castaneda, M. L. Peters, & X. Zúniga (Eds.), *Readings for diversity and social justice* (pp. 141–156). New York, NY: Routledge.

Tronco, J. D., Ramirez, A. M., Baggini, C. S., & Cervantes, R. M. (2013). *La violencia en las escuelas secundarias de México. Una exploración de sus dimensiones*. Mexico: FLACSO.

Velasco, C. N. (2016a). Las posiciones de las iglesias frente a la mujer. *La Manzana de la Discordia, 1*(1), 113–117.

Velasco, S. C. (2016b). Racismo y educación en México. *Revista Mexicana de Ciencias Políticas y Sociales, 61*(226), 379–407.

Valdés-Rodríguez, O. A., Palacios-Wassenaar, O. M., & Sánchez-Cruz, É. (2017). Los postgrados y su contribución al desarrollo de la ciencia en México: una perspectiva deinvestigadoras veracruzanas. *Revista Internacional de Desarrollo Regional Sustentable, 2*(1–2), 1–19.

Valdez, A. (2018). "Mamá luchona," la burla a las madres solteras. *Las Protagonistas. Periodismo con Perspectia de Género*. Retrieved June 9, 2019, from https://billieparkernoticias.com/mama-luchona-la-burla-a-las-madres-solteras/

Villaseñor-Farías, M., & Castañeda-Torres, J. D. (2003). Masculinidad, sexualidad, poder y violencia: analisis de significados en adolescentes. *Salud Publica de Mexico, 45*, S44–S57.

Yankelevich, P. (2017). Migración, mestizaje y xenofobia en México (1910–1950). *Anuario de Historia de América Latina, 54*, 129–156.

Zárate, R. (2017). We are Mexicans, we are not Blacks: Educating to make "anti-Black" racism visible. *Revista Latinoamericana de Educación Inclusiva, 11*(1), 57–72.

www.ingramcontent.com/pod-product-compliance
Lightning Source LLC
Chambersburg PA
CBHW021132300426
44113CB00006B/399